PRINCE VALIANT

FANTAGRAPHICS BOOKS 7563 Lake City Way NE, Seattle, WA 98115. Edited by Kim Thompson. Design by Adam Grano. Production by Paul Baresh. Promotion by Eric Reynolds. Gary Groth and Kim Thompson, publishers. Original scans for all *Prince Valiant* strips provided by The Special Collections Center of the Syracuse University Library. Images in introduction provided by Brian M. Kane. All comics material © 2010 King Features Syndicate, and introduction © 2010 Mark Schultz; remaining contents and this edition as a whole copyright © 2010 Fantagraphics Books, Inc. All rights reserved. Permission to quote or reproduce material for reviews or notices must be obtained from Fantagraphics Books, in writing, at 7563 Lake City Way NE, Seattle, WA 98115. Distributed in the U.S. by W.W. Norton and Company, Inc. (212-354-5500). Distributed in Canada by Canadian Manda Group (416-516-0911). Distributed in the United Kingdom by Turnaround Distribution (208-829-3009). First edition: March, 2010. ISBN: 978-1-60699-348-4. Printed in China. ✠✠✠

PRINCE VALIANT

VOL. 2: 1939-1940 — BY HAL FOSTER

PUBLISHED BY FANTAGRAPHICS BOOKS, INC., SEATTLE.

YES, HE WAS A CARTOONIST

Foreword by Mark Schultz

Hal Foster's enduring status as the most important figure in the development of adventure comic strips would be difficult to dispute: With *Tarzan,* his groundbreaking adaptation of Edgar Rice Burroughs' iconic ape man, and then *Prince Valiant,* his personal invention and masterpiece, Foster virtually single-handedly invented the visual language and set the storytelling standards that would dominate serial comic-strip adventure for decades. What is open to argument, however, is whether Foster was primarily a cartoonist, working with and exploiting the opportunities unique to the sequential medium — or more of a traditional illustrator squatting on the comics page while remaining largely aloof from comics conventions.

The distinction, of course, isn't that simple. Foster was very conscious of the differences in the disciplines and venues for which they were intended, and he made choices. Which elements of illustration Foster brought to the comics page, which illustrative elements he chose to abandon and which elements he incorporated from established color comics added up to a singular whole that made his work uniquely appealing, innovative and influential.

As with all accomplished storytellers, Foster's main goal was to tell his story as best he could, using the medium he was working within to its best advantage. It's true that he helped introduce illustrative aesthetics to the comic strips, but it is also important to note that he realized the limits as to how they could be applied to the sequential medium. He adapted them to work in four-color newsprint.

Foster, of course, began his career as a traditionally trained illustrator, first depicting retail catalogue items, later painting for editorial and advertising venues. Stylistically, he was squarely within the early 20th century American school, probably best exemplified by Howard Pyle and his Brandywine students. He only fell into comics work through financial necessity and, as he himself admitted, he didn't think much of the medium at first, only warming up to its possibilities in the face of positive fan reaction to his early work on *Tarzan.*

Tarzan was important as one of the first strips to attempt a dramatic adventure storyline *sans* humor. While it's arguable that there were legitimate predecessors to his approach (episodes of Roy Crane's *Capt. Easy* most obviously pointed the way), Foster was undeniably the first to bring to the comics page naturalistic (if heroic) proportions, deep perspective and an astonishing degree of realist detail in support of his narrative aims.

Understand, I'm throwing out "naturalistic" and "realist" cautiously — I use the terms relatively, to contrast Foster's draftsmanship with the much more expressionistic, caricature-oriented drawing styles that dominated the comics medium up to Foster's arrival. The fact is, there is nothing "naturalistic" or "realist" about black lines enclosing, or surrounded by, flat fields of color. Our eyes perceive the world through subtle tonal shifts over great changes in depth. By any stretch, all graphic comic strip work, even Foster's, is a highly abstracted translation of reality, relying on the human mind's ability to interpret two-dimensional symbols to something relatable in three-dimensional, "real" space. Foster's skill at reinterpreting the world into something flat and graphic yet completely understandable to the viewer

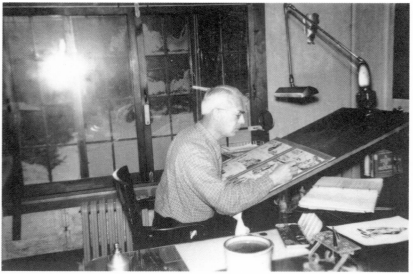

make him, as well as all accomplished graphic artists, an adept abstractionist. There really is a very small cognitive jump between the apparently dissimilar worlds depicted in *Prince Valiant* and, say, *Peanuts*, as compared with the chasm between either of those strips and our visually perceived reality.

But — Foster's figures, as well as the environments in which he set them, were proportioned and constructed much closer to the proportions, textures and details found in the natural world, as compared to the figures and environments presented throughout the greater comics page universe. His *relatively* naturalistic approach turned out to be perfect for use in the adventure strip, in which a sense of shared danger was required between character and reader. The reader could identify with the drama surrounding characters designed according to anatomical proportions similar to his — or, at least, proportions heroically extrapolated from his. This, joined with Foster's astonishing ability to convey emotion through carefully observed and translated facial and body expression, contributed greatly in creating a compelling story. Foster's vision and methods attracted an enthusiastic readership and a market for the adventure serial. He prepared the way for a flood of new comics exploiting dramatic avenues.

Foster, trained as an illustrator, was particularly adept at depicting human anatomy. A careful observer, he was also skilled at detailing natural and manufactured environments. His experiences adventuring in the wilds of Canada and his labors reproducing mundane household items for the Hudson Bay Company catalogue served him equally well. He brought all these talents to bear on his work in comics — anyone who has even casually paged through *Tarzan* or *Prince Valiant* has to admit that the man could convincingly draw anything to which he put his mind. His depictions of edged weapon combat, interpersonal intrigue and wilderness survival technique all come with an air of authenticity that springs from his working knowledge of the real world, and so allows the reader to invest his belief.

But bringing classically trained draftsmanship to the strips did not mean that Foster also brought along illustrative rendering.

This is where I think that those who consider Foster primarily an *illustrator* slumming in the comics make a wrong turn: Foster clearly distinguished between which elements of illustration worked on the comics page and which elements did not. He made conscious, reasoned aesthetic choices, the most obvious being to dump the traditional complexity of illustrative ink and pen line-work in favor of a simplified, outline and high-contrast style — all the better to tell the story.

The limits of time in producing a strip on deadline were, no doubt, part of his consideration in simplifying his ink rendering technique. But I believe Foster

also recognized an aesthetic advantage inherent in dispensing with line work aimed at creating tonality in favor of opening up space to the exploitation of color possibilities. I'm sure he also recognized the limitations of newspaper printing for reproducing delicate line work, as well as the danger of overloading complex, multi-panel pages with too much linear busyness.

From the very beginning of his comics career, adapting *Tarzan of the Apes* as a black and white daily strip, his inks — applied with both brush and pen — were consciously simplified and cast largely in high-contrast values. His work is meticulously designed with carefully spotted areas of bold blacks leading the eye through the sparely placed, delicately rendered passages. Foster largely dispensed with tone-building inking techniques, such as hatching, in favor of solid blacks which read very well on the dense comics page and, by the time he had settled in on *Prince Valiant*, served to showcase and offset his fine color arrangements. There is an art to making color work on top of black ink and Foster combined the two spectacularly well. His conservative line expertly frames fields of color where necessary and is left absent where advantageous. His generously distributed

blacks enhance the surrounding colors and make them sparkle.

Illustration influenced, tonal ink work applied with a pen nib was a common comic strip rendering method well into the 1930s. Comics artists with traditional illustration background, such as Frank Godwin (*Connie* and later *Rusty Riley*), as well as pure cartoonists working more expressionistically, such as George Herriman (*Krazy Kat*) and Billy De Beck (*Barney Google*), frequently filled panels with elaborate, tonal inking. Foster, even with his illustration background, moved away from this accepted mannerism and into something both naturalistic and allowing for experimentation with the unique color opportunities available on the comics page.

By the time he began *Prince Valiant*, Foster seemed ready to explore the possibilities presented by four-color printing. The printing method, which allowed the inexpensive reproduction of color in coordination with black line, had aesthetic origins in the ukiyo-e prints of Japan. When those pop culture artifacts had

FACING PAGE: *Hal Foster at his drawing table.* ABOVE: *A Foster illustration from the January, 1936 issue of* Popular Mechanics.

been introduced to Europe in the mid-nineteenth century, their non-Western presentation of color and composition became a huge influence on the artists moving beyond Academy restrictions. In America, Winslow Homer, both illustrator and landscapist, and a seminal influence on the Brandywine artists, incorporated ukiyo-e compositional experimentation into his paintings. But ukiyo-e itself was intrinsically a graphic medium — created for cheap, mass reproduction. As such, it was recognized and absorbed into American newsprint: The printing of color in conjunction with black line as used in the American Sunday strip is the direct descendent of the ukiyo-e aesthetic. In the heyday of four-color printing — when print engravers were master craftsmen — great expression was possible with this relatively crude process. Foster saw the opportunities, quite divorced from his background in traditional Western illustration, and took full advantage.

Many other strip artists had already explored the dramatic possibilities offered by four-color process — Crane, Lyonel Feininger, Cliff Sterrett and Frank King come to mind — but Foster pushed his color use in context with his classically naturalistic draftsmanship, enhancing his perspectives and material textures, and creating intensely emotional atmospheres. To best incorporate the advantages of the process, he reduced his illustrative line work, often dropping the line altogether, allowing color fields to float free and recess into the picture plain, and made his spotted blacks bolder, all in service of evoking a mood, conveying technical information and, ultimately, advancing the story. From this volume alone, the contents of which represent a period when Foster's work was beginning to hit its full, mature stride, any single panel might serve as an example of his brilliant color use. But, for examples of the wide-ranging uses to which he put color, take a peek at strip #103, panel 4; #127, panels 5 and 6; #157, panel 4; #182, panel 4; #184, panel 1 and #185, panel 2. In every panel, the color scheme is not just decorative — it is chosen to convey very specific information, to advance or enhance the reader's appreciation of the story.

All these considerations helped Foster to compress an incredible amount of information — far more than any other comics work before or since, I'd argue — into his weekly page. Information in comics, conveyed in the interrelated, sequential packets called panels, must be presented within a finite amount of space. There is only so much real estate in which to deliver the information chosen to best convey the story to the reader. Foster wrought an incredible amount of story out of every square inch of real estate. The simplification of his ink line helped make this possible — too much fancy ink filigree would have been visually fatiguing, used in panel after panel. By eliminating unnecessary rendering, he left room for denser amounts of story information, presented with rigorous clarity. His thoughtful use of black spotting and color also served him well in this regard.

There was one other creative choice Foster made that most clearly separates him from the greater body of cartoonists — Foster presented his strips' texts in the form of open captions, with narration and dialogue intermixed. He dispensed with one of the strip cartoonists' unique tools, the word balloon. A singular stylistic choice, it's impossible to imagine *Prince Valiant* otherwise, so completely is this uncommon feature integrated into the formal look of the strip. I have no idea whether or not the decision owes any allegiance on Foster's part to book illustration, but the conceit does work well to consolidate textual information and

organize the panels, with their big dollops of visual information, into easily read designs. Word balloons would have made *Valiant* a different experience, read in a very different rhythm.

I dwell on all these technical points only in an attempt to help understand the nuts and bolts, the foundations, which supported Foster's extraordinarily effective storytelling. *Prince Valiant* remains popular to this day (despite Foster's own cautious estimation) not because of any of the specific graphic elements I've outlined, but because those elements gave his sequential storytelling a power and attraction that continues to resonate decades later. The fact that we have this beautiful new presentation of his *magnum opus* attests to the strip's continued ability to capture an audience beyond the usual circle of classic comics aficionados. Readers of Foster's *Prince Valiant* certainly respond to his illustrative, relatable draftsmanship, but that in and of itself is not enough to explain its continued popularity. The strip has been followed for decades and continues to attract new fans because Foster's formidable graphic skills and tricks were carefully weighed for their ability to help create memorable characters, real emotion and gripping stories. Foster was a world-class storyteller who understood his medium, top to bottom. ✣

The creator of the Eisner and Harvey Award-winning comic book Xenozoic Tales *(a.k.a.* Cadillacs and Dinosaurs), *Mark Schultz has been writing the weekly syndicated* Prince Valiant *strip since November of 2004.* Prince Valiant: Far From Camelot *(2008, Andrews McMeel) collects the first three and a half years of Schultz's* Valiant, *as illustrated by Gary Gianni.*

LEFT: *Original Foster drawing for a toy crossbow ad.*
ABOVE: *Foster remained an avid outdoorsman and hunter for most of his life.*

THE LADY OF THE LAKE
SAVE THIS STAMP

Prince Valiant

IN THE DAYS OF KING ARTHUR
BY HAROLD R FOSTER

Registered U. S. Patent Office

LEODEGRANCE
FATHER OF GUINEVERE
SAVE THIS STAMP

SYNOPSIS: WHEN PRINCE VALIANT DASHES INTO CAMELOT WITH NEWS OF A SAXON INVASION KING ARTHUR IMMEDIATELY CALLS THE GRAND COUNCIL OF WAR INTO SESSION. VAL'S HASTE HAS EXHAUSTED HIS OWN HORSE AND HE FINDS IT NECESSARY TO STEAL A LADY'S PALFREY TO FINISH HIS JOURNEY AND HAS BEEN PURSUED ALL THE WAY BY HER ENRAGED HUSBAND, WHO, IN HIS ANGER, FORGETS ALL ABOUT HIS ABANDONED WIFE......

AN HOUR LATER AND INTO CAMELOT COMES THE FUMING LADY, DESERTED IN THE FOREST, RIDING ASTRIDE A MAN'S SADDLE, HER DIGNITY HURT.....

AS HIS ANGER COOLED SIR KNIGHT BETHINKS HIM OF THE WIFE HE HAS ABANDONED IN THE FOREST — BUT TOO LATE.

NOW, WHEN A LONG-SUFFERING WIFE, WHO HAS WORKED HER FINGERS TO THE BONE FOR AN UNAPPRECIATIVE HUSBAND, FEELS IT HER DUTY TO GIVE THE WRETCH A GOOD TALKING TO — FOR HIS OWN GOOD, OF COURSE....

.....AND THE SIGHT OF HIM IN COMPANY WITH A HORSE-THIEF REMINDS HER OF OTHER THINGS THAT SHOULD BE MENTIONED.....

.....NOT EVEN THE ANNOYANCE OF A KING CAN HALT THE FLOW OF REALLY CONSTRUCTIVE CRITICISM!

SOFTLY KING ARTHUR DRAWS THE CURTAINS — "LET US HASTEN OUR PLANS THAT WE MAY FIND THE COMPARATIVE PEACE OF THE BATTLE-FIELD!" (FOR HE, TOO, IS A MARRIED MAN).

AND SO THE COUNCIL RESUMES ITS PLANS FOR THE TENTH WAR AGAINST THE SAXONS.

"THEY HARBOR IN THE FENS," SAYS MERLIN, "WHO KNOWS AUGHT OF THESE WASTES?" THEN ARISES SIR GAWAIN, "NO ONE IN ALL ENGLAND KNOWS THEM AS DOES PRINCE VALIANT."

Cpr. 1938, King Features Syndicate, Inc., World rights reserved. 99 1-1-39

AND SO VAL IS SUMMONED TO KING ARTHUR'S COUNCIL OF WAR.

·NEXT WEEK·
BATTLE PLANS

KNIGHT'S HEAD ARMOR — SAVE THIS STAMP

Prince Valiant

IN THE DAYS OF KING ARTHUR BY HAROLD R. FOSTER

FOOT SOLDIER LEATHER HELMET — SAVE THIS STAMP

SYNOPSIS: PRINCE VALIANT DISCOVERS A VAST FLEET OF SAXON SHIPS AND SPEEDS TO CAMELOT WITH THE NEWS — THE KING CALLS A COUNCIL OF WAR BUT NONE KNOWS THE GREAT MARSHES WHERE THE FLEET LIES.

SO VAL IS CALLED AND FOR THE FIRST TIME A HUMBLE SQUIRE BECOMES ONE OF THE GRAND COUNCIL.

"PRINCE VALIANT, YOU HAVE LIVED IN THE FENS, TELL US ALL YOU KNOW OF THE INVADERS' POSITION AND HOW WE CAN MEET THEM."

TAKING A CHARRED STICK FROM THE FIREPLACE, VAL STEPS UPON A TABLE AND DRAWS A MAP OF THE FENS ON THE WALL.

"THEIR FLEET NUMBERS 300 SHIPS AND ABOUT 20,000 MEN, THEY LIE IN A BAY SURROUNDED BY TALL REEDS AND CAN LAND ON EITHER SHORE."

AND LISTENING TO THE YOUNG WARRIOR'S WORDS ARE THE GREAT NOBLES OF THE KING'S COUNCIL OF WAR —
FIRST, WISE MERLIN
LAUNCELOT, THE COURTEOUS
MIGHTY TRISTRAM
ULFIUS AND BRASTIAS, THE EVER FAITHFUL
BEDIVERE, WHO SERVED HIS KING TO THE END
KAY, THE SENESCHAL
GAWAIN, THE LIGHT-HEARTED
SIR MODRED, WHO LATER BECOMES A TRAITOR
SIR ECTOR, KING'S GUARDIAN.

100 1-8-39

SHIELD — SAVE THIS STAMP

"SIRE, THE SAXONS NUMBER 20,000, WE CAN MUSTER BUT 10,000 IN TIME TO OPPOSE A LANDING — TO DEFEND BOTH SHORES WOULD SPLIT OUR ARMY AND WEAKEN IT, OUR SHIPS ARE TOO FEW — BUT I HAVE A PLAN."

WITH THE KING'S PERMISSION THE DARING LAD UNFOLDS AN IMPISH SCHEME OF SUCH AUDACITY THAT THE NOBLE LORDS OF THE COUNCIL SHOUT WITH APPROVAL.

Copr. 1939, King Features Syndicate, Inc., World rights reserved.

THEN FROM THE SEVEN GATES OF CAMELOT SPEED THE KING'S COURIERS TO SUMMON ALL TO WAR!

—NEXT WEEK—
THE SMOKE SCREEN

HAL FOSTER

SWORD HILT FORMING A CROSS BEFORE WHICH THE KNIGHT PRAYED AT SUNSET — SAVE THIS STAMP

YEOMAN
SAVE THIS STAMP

Prince Valiant

Registered U. S. Patent Office.

IN THE DAYS OF
KING ARTHUR
BY
HAROLD R. FOSTER

PIKEMAN
SAVE THIS STAMP

SYNOPSIS: TO DELAY THE LANDING OF THE INVADING SAXON ARMY VAL AROUSED THE FENS' PEOPLE TO HAMPER THE SCOUTS. THE PLAN HE SUBMITTED TO THE KING HAS BEEN ACCEPTED AND THE KNIGHTS OF ENGLAND GATHER TO DEFEND THE REALM.

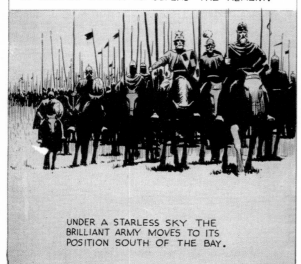

UNDER A STARLESS SKY THE BRILLIANT ARMY MOVES TO ITS POSITION SOUTH OF THE BAY.

AT DAWN HORSA, THE SAXON CHIEFTAN, POINTS NORTHWARD TO THE LEVEL PLAIN. "THE BRITONS GATHER THERE, FOR I SEE THE DRAGON HELMET OF ARTHUR AND THE LION SHIELDS OF LAUNCELOT AND TRISTRAM!"

BUT THE FACE OF DAGONET, THE JESTER, LOOKS OUT FROM BENEATH THE KING'S GOLDEN CASQUE AND A SCULLERY LAD AND A STABLE BOY CARRY THE SHIELDS OF LAUNCELOT AND TRISTRAM.

"THEY WISH US TO THINK THE ARMY AWAITS US ON THE SOUTH — BUT WE ARE NOT FOOLED — THOSE ARE BUT DUMMIES."

BUT BEHIND THE DUMMIES THE GLITTERING ARMY AWAITS VAL'S SIGNAL.

THE KING'S SCANTY FLEET, WAITING OUT-SIDE THE BAY, IS GREETED WITH DERISION.

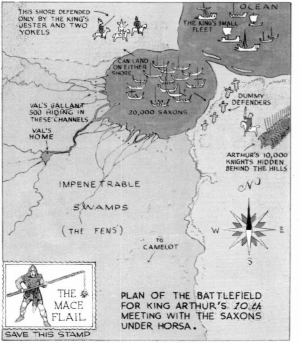

THIS SHORE DEFENDED ONLY BY THE KING'S JESTER AND TWO YOKELS

OCEAN

THE KING'S SMALL FLEET

CAN LAND ON EITHER SHORE

20,000 SAXONS

DUMMY DEFENDERS

VAL'S GALLANT 500 HIDING IN THESE CHANNELS

VAL'S HOME

ARTHUR'S 10,000 KNIGHTS HIDDEN BEHIND THE HILLS

N
W E
S

IMPENETRABLE

SWAMPS

(THE FENS)

TO CAMELOT

THE MACE FLAIL
SAVE THIS STAMP

PLAN OF THE BATTLEFIELD FOR KING ARTHUR'S *10th* MEETING WITH THE SAXONS UNDER HORSA.

NEXT WEEK — THE BATTLE   101 1-15-39

.....AND NOW, — DOWN THE TOR-TUOUS CHANNELS OF THE GREAT SWAMP MOVES A STRANGE FLEET LOADED WITH FIRE-BALLS AND BOUND ON A DARING MISSION.

HAL FOSTER

REPELLING HORSEMEN
SAVE THIS STAMP

FIRE-THROWER

LEATHER ARMOR
SAVE THIS STAMP

FIRE-BALL
WITH GRAPPLES
SAVE THIS STAMP

SYNOPSIS: NEVER HAS SUCH A GREAT SAXON FORCE INVADED BRITAIN — AND NEVER IN A STRONGER POSITION. IN DESPERATION THE KING ADOPTS THE MAD, INGENIOUS PLAN THAT VAL UNFOLDS TO THE GRAND COUNCIL OF WAR. VAL HAS PROMISED THAT, WITH 500 MEN, HE WILL DRIVE 20,000 ARMED SAXON WARRIORS IN PANIC BEFORE ARTHUR'S WAITING ARMY.

VAL SHOUTS A COMMAND, A TRUMPET SOUNDS AND IN A MOMENT THE MARSH IS A MASS OF FLAMES.

THE ASTONISHED SAXONS SEE THE BAY QUICKLY ENCIRCLED ON THREE SIDES BY A LEAPING SHEET OF FLAME — THEN SUDDENLY THEY ARE ENVELOPED IN A DENSE CLOUD OF CHOKING SMOKE.

AND OUT OF THAT SMOKE COMES A SHOWER OF FIRE-BALLS THROWN BY AN INVISIBLE ENEMY!

BURNING RAFTS AND FLAMING CANOES DRIFT WITH THE WIND AMONG THE ANCHORED SHIPS ..... FIRE AND CONFUSION ARE EVERYWHERE.

"TO SHORE," SCREAMS HORSA, "THE SOUTH BANK IS DEFENDED ONLY BY DUMMIES, LAND THERE AND REORGANIZE."

102 1-22-39

VAL HEARS THE COMMAND AND IMMEDIATELY CHANGES HIS ATTACK.

CAST IRON
FIREPOT
SAVE THIS STAMP

AS THE SAXONS LAND TO REFORM THEIR RANKS A DEADLY SHOWER OF ARROWS COMES OUT OF THE SMOKE AND DRIVES THEM INLAND.

Copr. 1939, King Features Syndicate, Inc. World rights reserved

THE INVADERS COME STUMBLING OUT FROM BENEATH THE CLOUD OF STIFLING SMOKE AND STINGING ARROWS AND THERE — DRAWN UP IN BATTLE ARRAY, IS THE KING'S ARMY!

· NEXT WEEK ·
PRINCE VALIANT
IS KNIGHTED!

HAL FOSTER

SAVE THIS STAMP

WHIP MACE

THE KING'S JESTER
DAGONET
SAVE THIS STAMP

Prince Valiant

IN THE DAYS OF
KING ARTHUR
BY
HAROLD R FOSTER

Registered U. S. Patent Office.

THE KIN
THE ARMORER
SAVE THIS STAMP

SYNOPSIS: WITH BUT 10,000 MEN KING ARTHUR FACES AN ARMY OF 20,000 SAXON WARRIORS. VAL PROMISES TO DELIVER THE INVADERS IN PANIC BEFORE THE KING'S MEN AND, WITH FLAME, SMOKE AND ARROWS, KEEPS HIS PROMISE.

MIGHTY ARE THE DEEDS OF LAUNCELOT, GREAT IS TRISTRAM WITH SWORD AND SHIELD, BUT NONE IS TERRIBLE AS ARTHUR WHEN THEY CHARGE INTO BATTLE SHOUTING!

ON THE BAY AMID THE FLAME AND SMOKE PRINCE VAL AND HIS NIMBLE BAND COMPLETE THE DESTRUCTION OF THE FLEET.

THOSE SHIPS THAT GROPED THEIR WAY OUT THROUGH THE SMOKE FIND THE KING'S FLEET AWAITING THEM.

103 1-29-39

FINALLY THE SHATTERED ARMY IS NO MORE AND THAT AWFUL DAY DRAWS TO A CLOSE. AMID THE BLOODY WRECKAGE OF WAR KING ARTHUR WAITS WHILE A BURNED AND BLACKENED TROOP COMES SLOWLY UP FROM THE BAY.

KING RYONS
OF IRELAND
SAVE THIS STAMP

VAL STANDS BEFORE THE KING. "ONE DEED IS YET TO BE DONE THIS DAY—KNEEL," SAYS ARTHUR DRAWING KEEN EXCALIBUR FROM ITS JEWELLED SCABBARD AND TOUCHING THE GRIMY LAD UPON THE SHOULDER, "NOW RISE, SIR VALIANT, PRINCE AND KNIGHT OF THE ROUND TABLE!"

HAL FOSTER

NEXT WEEK:
NEW KINGDOMS

Copr. 1939, King Features Syndicate, Inc., World rights reserved

LILE OF AVELION
SAVE THIS STAMP

MOTHER OF ARTHUR · IGRAINE · SAVE THIS STAMP

Prince Valiant

IN THE DAYS OF KING ARTHUR
BY HAROLD R FOSTER

Registered U. S. Patent Office

FATHER OF ARTHUR · UTHER PENDRAGON · SAVE THIS STAMP

SYNOPSIS: THE SUN SINKS BLOOD-RED BEHIND THE SMOKE OF THE BURNING FLEET AND VICTORIOUS ARTHUR GATHERS HIS HOSTS ABOUT HIM..... AND THERE, AMID THE WRECKAGE OF THAT TERRIBLE FIELD, HE MAKES PRINCE VALIANT A KNIGHT OF THE ROUND TABLE!

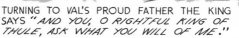

TURNING TO VAL'S PROUD FATHER THE KING SAYS "AND YOU, O RIGHTFUL KING OF THULE, ASK WHAT YOU WILL OF ME."

"ONLY ONE OF THE SHIPS WE HAVE CAPTURED THAT WE MAY SAIL ONCE AGAIN TO THULE."

"I HAD FORESEEN YOUR REQUEST, FATHER, AND WAS CAREFUL TO PRESERVE YONDER GOODLY SHIP FROM THE FLAMES."

AS THEY DRESS THEIR BURNS AND WOUNDS AND WASH AWAY THE GRIME OF BATTLE, THE OLD WARRIORS ARE HAPPY IN THE THOUGHT THAT SOON THEY WILL SAIL FOR HOME.

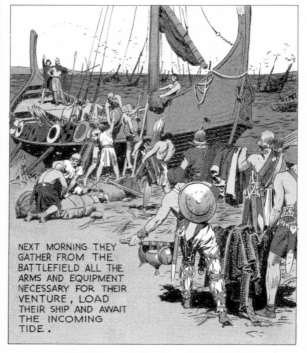

NEXT MORNING THEY GATHER FROM THE BATTLEFIELD ALL THE ARMS AND EQUIPMENT NECESSARY FOR THEIR VENTURE, LOAD THEIR SHIP AND AWAIT THE INCOMING TIDE.

UP THE TWISTING CHANNELS THEY WORK THE SHIP TO THE ISLAND THAT HAS BEEN THEIR HOME DURING 12 YEARS OF EXILE.

MORGAN LE FEY · SISTER OF ARTHUR · SAVE THIS STAMP

THE FINAL PREPARATIONS ARE COMPLETED — THEN HO! FOR THE OPEN SEA!

BEHIND LIES PEACE AND SAFETY IN BRITAIN; AHEAD IS THE UNHAPPY LAND OF THULE IN THE GRIP OF SLIGON, THE TYRANT; DANGER, AND PERHAPS DEATH. BUT TWENTY KEEN SWORDS AND TWENTY STOUT HEARTS ARE PLEDGED TO REGAIN A KINGDOM AND THEIR HOMES.

·NEXT WEEK· THE CRUSADE

SIR MORDRED · SON OF LE FEY · SAVE THIS STAMP

Prince Valiant

Registered U. S. Patent Office.

IN THE DAYS OF
KING ARTHUR
BY
HAROLD R. FOSTER

SYNOPSIS: FOR HIS SPLENDID DEEDS IN BATTLE PRINCE VALIANT IS MADE KNIGHT OF THE ROUND TABLE AND GRANTED A SHIP IN WHICH TO SAIL FOR THULE. THEY PLEDGE THEMSELVES TO BANISH THE TYRANT SLIGON AND PLACE VAL'S FATHER BACK ON HIS THRONE.

AT LAST THEY SEE THE FAIR SHORE OF THEIR HOMELAND SPARKLING IN THE SUNLIGHT.

THEY LAND AND STORE THEIR GREAT CARGO OF ARMS IN A FRIENDLY VILLAGE.

THEN THE KING APPLIES A TORCH TO THE SHIP. "WE HAVE BEEN DRIVEN FROM THESE SHORES ONCE, BUT WE HAVE RETURNED NEVERMORE TO LEAVE. WE WILL BRING PEACE TO THE PEOPLE WE LOVE OR FIND PEACE BENEATH THE SOIL WE HONOR."

THEN COME BUSY, DANGEROUS DAYS; SWIFT MESSENGERS RIDING AT NIGHT CARRY TIDINGS OF THE KING'S RETURN.

THE FAITHFUL TWENTY RANGE FAR AND WIDE PROMISING THE ENSLAVED PEASANTS FREEDOM AND JUSTICE UNDER THE KING'S BANNER.

SLOWLY AT FIRST BUT IN EVER INCREASING NUMBERS, RESOLUTE MEN GATHER AT THE KING'S HIDING-PLACE AND ARE ARMED.

VAL, WORKING AMONG THE KNIGHTS AND WARRIORS, HAS MANY A FIGHT.

MANY OF THE NOBLES COME TO THE KING SECRETLY AND PLEDGE LOYALTY.

SLIGON'S SPIES HINDER, BUT CANNOT STOP THE GROWING REVOLT.

MADE BOLD BY HOPE OF DELIVERANCE THE VILLAGERS ATTACK SLIGON'S BRUTAL TAX-GATHERERS.

INTO THIS TROUBLED LAND THE BANNER OF THE RED STALLION COMES LIKE A RAY OF HOPE AND, AS THE DAYS SPEED SWIFTLY BY, THE KING'S CAUSE PROSPERS.

IN HIS CLOSE-GUARDED STRONGHOLD SLIGON BROODS, SICK IN MIND AND BODY, WHILE HIS EVIL POWER MELTS AWAY BEFORE THE EXILED KING'S PLEDGE, "FREEDOM AND JUSTICE!"
NEXT WEEK: "THE BARGAIN"

105 2-12-39

Prince Valiant

Registered U. S. Patent Office.

IN THE DAYS OF KING ARTHUR.
BY HAROLD R. FOSTER

SYNOPSIS: FOR TWELVE LONG YEARS THE PEOPLE OF THULE HAVE SUFFERED UNDER THE TYRANNY OF SLIGON, SO WHEN THEIR EXILED KING RETURNS IN SECRET AND RAISES ONCE MORE THE BANNER OF THE RED STALLION THEY FLOCK TO HIS SUPPORT UNTIL HIS STRENGTH SOON EQUALS THAT OF SLIGON.

SLIGON'S SOLDIERS ARE CALLED IN TO PROTECT HIS STRONGHOLD.

AND NOW THE HOUR HAS COME! THE KING PREPARES TO MARCH.

BUT A MESSENGER GALLOPS UP CRYING, "SLIGON WILL DISCUSS TERMS WITH PRINCE VALIANT AND GUARANTEE HIS SAFETY IF HE DARE COME."

THE COUNCIL, WELL-USED TO SLIGON'S TREACHERY, ADVISE AGAINST IT, BUT VAL DECIDES TO GO ON THE OFF CHANCE THAT SOMEHOW THE MEN OF THULE MAY BE SAVED A RUINOUS WAR.

ALONE HE ENTERS THE ENEMY FORTRESS; A CASTLE HE ONCE CALLED HOME.

HAL FOSTER

"THE KINGDOM OF THULE I TOOK BY FORCE; BY FORCE I HAVE HELD IT, BUT I WEARY OF FORCE, OF CRUELTY, TREACHERY AND DISTRUST. ABOUT ME ARE FAWNING COURTIERS WITH FLATTERING WORDS ON THEIR TONGUES AND HATRED IN THEIR EYES AND I FEAR THESE SILKEN JACKALS — GO TO YOUR FATHER AND SAY: 'SLIGON IS BUT A TIRED HUCKSTER AT HEART AND WILL BARTER THE KINGDOM OF THULE FOR HIS PEACEFUL ISLAND IN THE ENGLISH SWAMPS'."

NEXT WEEK: **"VICTORY"**

THE CROWN OF THULE — SAVE THIS STAMP

Prince Valiant

IN THE DAYS OF KING ARTHUR
BY
HAROLD R FOSTER

Registered U. S. Patent Office.

CHALICE OF THE KING — SAVE THIS STAMP

SYNOPSIS: SLIGON WAS ONCE A MIGHTY TYRANT, BUT NOW, WEARY AND SICK, HE OFFERS HIS TOTTERING THRONE TO THE KING IN EXCHANGE FOR A TINY, PEACEFUL ISLAND IN THE QUIET ENGLISH SWAMPS.

WITH THIS WELCOME NEWS VAL GALLOPS TO HIS FATHER'S CAMP AND THE BARGAIN IS MADE AMID GREAT REJOICING.

AS THE RIGHTFUL KING ONCE MORE ENTERS THE GREAT FORTRESS WHERE HE AND HIS FATHERS BEFORE HIM HAD RULED WITH FIRM JUSTICE, SLIGON SLIPS UNNOTICED FROM ANOTHER GATE TO FIND THE PEACE AND QUIET HE HAS NEVER KNOWN.

IN THE PALACE THE KING PLUNGES INTO THE WORK OF REORGANIZING THE HARSH GOVERNMENT AND SMOOTHING OUT OLD INJUSTICES.

TO PRINCE VALIANT FALLS THE TASK OF BRINGING INTO LINE ALL THOSE NOBLES WHO HAVE NOT YET PLEDGED FEALTY TO THE KING.

IN THESE ROUGH DAYS THERE IS BUT ONE WAY TO SETTLE A DISPUTE— THE TRIAL BY ARMS.

HAPPY DAYS FOR A HIGH-HEARTED YOUNG WARRIOR! AMID THE THUNDER OF HOOFS AND THE CLASH OF ARMS HE BRINGS TO MANY A DESIRE FOR PEACE AND QUIET - AT ANY PRICE.

BUT WHEN SLIGON SAID HE WANTED PEACE HE WAS SINCERE - SO SINCERE IN FACT THAT HE LEAVES HIS WIFE AND DAUGHTER BEHIND.

107 2-26-39

THE BUSY KING PROVIDES THEM WITH APARTMENTS IN A DISTANT WING OF THE CASTLE AND THEN FORGETS THEM, BUT CLARIS IS NOT THE KIND OF GIRL ONE CAN FORGET FOR LONG.

NEXT WEEK "CLARIS"

Hal Foster

SLIGON
SAVE THIS STAMP

Prince Valiant

IN THE DAYS OF
KING ARTHUR
BY
HAROLD R FOSTER

Registered U. S. Patent Office.

CLARIS
SAVE THIS STAMP

SYNOPSIS: THE VICTORIOUS KING PROVIDES SLIGON'S ABANDONED WIFE AND DAUGHTER WITH APARTMENTS IN A DISTANT WING OF THE CASTLE AND THEN PROCEEDS TO FORGET ABOUT THEM — BUT PRETTY CLARIS IS NOT ONE TO BE FORGOTTEN FOR LONG.

FOR CLARIS IS AN ARTFUL LITTLE IMP WHO HAS TROUBLED MANY HEARTS — BY WAY OF PRACTICE.

SO WHEN, FROM HER TOWER, SHE SEES PRINCE VALIANT RETURNING SHE TIDIES HER HAIR, PUTS ON HER MOST BECOMING GOWN AND SMILES A THOUGHTFUL SMILE.

FOR VAL IS RETURNING FROM A SIX-MONTHS TOUR OF THE KINGDOM, DURING WHICH HE HAS WON MANY OF SLIGON'S OLD SUPPORTERS OVER TO HIS FATHER'S CAUSE.

NOT WITH FAIR WORDS AND PROMISES, FOR VAL FOUND HE COULD BETTER POINT OUT THEIR ERRORS WITH A LANCE AND DRIVE HOME AN ARGUMENT WITH A SWORD.

IT HAPPENS, JUST BY THE ODDEST CHANCE IMAGINABLE, THAT THESE TWO MEET IN THE GARDEN.

IT IS PLEASANT, AFTER ALL THESE MONTHS OF FIGHTING AND HARDSHIP, TO BE AT EASE IN A SUNNY GARDEN WITH SO GAY A COMPANION.

SO THESE TWO YOUNG PEOPLE ARE OFTEN TOGETHER — HE LIKES HER MERRY WIT AND READY LAUGHTER — AND SHE IS CAREFUL TO LOOK HER BEST.

VAL MAKES LIGHT-HEARTED LOVE TO HER, (FOR WHO WOULD BE SO UNGALLANT AS TO NEGLECT THE DUTY WE ALL OWE TO BEAUTIFUL LADIES?) BUT HE REFUSES TO TAKE HER SERIOUSLY, FOR THE MEMORY OF HIS TRAGIC ROMANCE WITH ILENE IS STILL FRESH IN HIS HEART. SHE USES ALL HER PRETTY ARTS TO NO AVAIL — IT IS MOST DISCOURAGING.

DE GERIN
ALFRED
SAVE THIS STAMP

ONE DAY CLARIS SEES VAL WITH HIS CLOSEST FRIEND, GOOD-NATURED ALFRED DE GERIN, AND SHE HAS AN IDEA — WHY NOT STIR VAL OUT OF HIS GAY INDIFFERENCE WITH JEALOUSY?

108 3-5-39

AND SO SHE STARTS A LITTLE FLIRTATION WITH SIMPLE ALFRED.

HAL FOSTER

INSTEAD OF KINDLING A SPARK IN PRINCE VALIANT SHE STARTS A RAGING FIRE IN THE HEART OF POOR INNOCENT ALFRED.

NEXT WEEK: "A CHALLENGE"

UNDEFEATED
CHAMPION

CROWN PRINCE VALIANT OF THULE, HOT-TEMPERED, LIGHT-HEARTED, BUT STILL BROODING OVER A TRAGIC ROMANCE, PROVES A DIFFICULT PROBLEM FOR·····

CLARIS WHO WISH-ES TO WED HIM AND BECOME THE FUTURE QUEEN OF THULE. SO FAR ALL HER ARTFUL WILES HAVE PROVED UNAVAILING···· ····SHE HAS EVEN TRIED TO AWAK-EN HIS JEALOUSY BY A MILD FLIRTATION WITH HIS FRIEND····

TALL ALFRED WHO PROMPTLY FALLS IN LOVE WITH THE SCHEMING LITTLE MINX, LOSING HIS HEART, HIS APPETITE AND HIS PEACE OF MIND.

SEEING VAL APPROACH, CLARIS PLAYS HER LITTLE GAME FOR HIS BENEFIT.

WITH ASTONISHING RESULTS — CLARIS FINDS HERSELF BEING THOROUGHLY, ARDENTLY AND DELIGHTFULLY KISSED.

VAL IS FURIOUS; "ALFRED, YOUR UNBECOMING CONDUCT DISPLEASES ME!" AND ALFRED, HIS HEAD WHIRL-ING, REPLIES, "YOU WILL FIND ME READY WHEN-EVER YOUR DISPLEASURE TAKES ACTIVE FORM."

CLARIS SITS DOWN·····SHE HAS BEEN KISSED BE-FORE, BUT NEVER QUITE SO EARNESTLY·····AND THAT TALL, BLUNDERING FOOL HAS UPSET HER PLANS, TOO·····HE IS A STUPID OX, EVEN IF HE DOES HAVE NICE EYES. SHE HATES HIM SO MUCH SHE RATHER SUSPECTS SHE IS FALL-ING IN LOVE WITH HIM.

THE TWO LADS ARM THEMSELVES AND REPAIR TO A WOOD — THERE TO SETTLE THE LITTLE MATTER OF THE STOLEN KISS.

POOR ALFRED — EVEN IF HE WINS THE DUEL THE KING WILL PROMPT-LY HANG HIM — CLARIS APPEALS TO THE KING.

THE TWO YOUNG WARRIORS ARE HACKING AT EACH OTHER WITH LUSTY ENTHUSIASM WHEN THE AN-GRY KING PUTS A STOP TO IT.   109   3-12-39

HE BELIEVES CLARIS TO BE A SCHEM-ING LITTLE TROUBLEMAKER AND TELLS VAL SO. VAL'S HOT TEMPER FLARES AND HE TELLS HIS FATHER HE WILL NOT BE BULLIED, EVEN BY A KING AND CAN VERY WELL LOOK AFTER HIS OWN AFFAIRS.

NEXT WEEK: "TANGLED AFFAIRS"

DANE
SAVE THIS STAMP

SOLDIER OF FAR CATHAY
SAVE THIS STAMP

SYNOPSIS: CLARIS, DAUGHTER OF SLIGON, IS AN AMBITIOUS LITTLE LADY WHO IS DETERMINED TO MARRY CROWN PRINCE VALIANT AND BECOME THE FUTURE QUEEN OF THULE, COST WHAT IT MAY. THE KING FORBIDS VAL TO HAVE ANYTHING TO DO WITH HER AND FATHER AND SON QUARREL.

"SINCE ILENE IS GONE AND I CAN NEVER LOVE AGAIN WHY NOT WED CLARIS? SHE IS PRETTY AND GAY AND WILL KEEP ME FROM BEING LONELY."

SO HE STRAIGHTWAY GOES TO CLARIS AND DEMANDS, "WILL YOU MARRY ME?" "YES", — AND THEN SHE LIES PRETTILY, "FOR I HAVE LOVED YOU FROM THE FIRST."
"FINE...I'LL HAVE HORSES READY AT DAWN FOR WE MUST FLEE THE ANGER OF THE KING."

"WE WILL SPEED TO BRITTANY. THERE WILL BE SOME SPLENDID FIGHTING UNDER KING BAN; THEN TO ENGLAND WITH KING ARTHUR, THERE SHOULD BE SOME SPLENDID BATTLES GOING ON EVEN NOW. OH, WE WILL BE HAPPY."

ONE BY ONE HER DREAM CASTLES TUMBLE ABOUT HER EARS. SHE WANTS TO MARRY A PRINCE, NOT A LIGHT-HEARTED BUTCHER. SHE WANTS TO SIT ON THE THRONE OF THULE, NOT ON A WAR-HORSE IN FOGGY ENGLAND. IN FACT, WHAT SHE WANTS MOST OF ALL, SHE DECIDES, IS TO BE LOVED BY · · · ·

· · · ALFRED, THAT BLUNDERING, TALL IDIOT, WHO HAS SPOILED ALL HER PLANS BY FALLING IN LOVE WITH HER AND KISSING HER SO ROUGHLY. SHE WONDERS IF HE WILL EVER LEARN ANY BETTER.

SHE GOES TO FIND OUT AND VAL LOOKING INTO THE SUNLIT GARDENS SEES THEM · · · · · LISTENING HE HEARS A SMALL VOICE WAILING · · · · ·

SAVE THIS STAMP
TARTAR

"I PROMISED AND I HAVE TO GO, I MAY BE QUEEN SOME DAY IF I DON'T CATCH MY DEATH OF COLD FOLLOWING VAL ALL OVER THOSE DRAUGHTY BATTLEFIELDS AND IT IS UNFAIR OF YOU TO BE SO HANDSOME."

"WELL, STRIKE ME WITH A BATTLE-AX! FATHER WAS RIGHT, THE LITTLE TRICKSTER! FANCY HER WANTING TO BE QUEEN OF THULE WHEN SHE CAN RULE THE HEART OF A LAD LIKE ALFRED... I'LL FIX HER."

Copr. 1939, King Features Syndicate, Inc., World rights reserved. 110 · 3-19-39

HAL FOSTER

POOR LOVELORN ALFRED IS ON THE BRINK OF DESPAIR WHEN VAL FINDS HIM AND UNFOLDS A LITTLE SCHEME.
NEXT WEEK: TRICKING A TRICKSTER

SAVE THIS STAMP
SELJUK TURK

GENSERIC 455 A.D. VANDAL KING
SAVE THIS STAMP

EMPEROR OF ROME 455 A.D. VALENTINIAN
SAVE THIS STAMP

SYNOPSIS: POOR LITTLE CLARIS, SHE WORKED AND SCHEMED SO CLEVERLY TO BECOME THE BRIDE OF PRINCE VALIANT AND THE FUTURE QUEEN OF THULE, ONLY TO FALL IN LOVE WITH THE LAD WHOSE HEART SHE HAS BROKEN, EARN THE DISPLEASURE OF THE KING AND BECOME PLEDGED TO ELOPE WITH VAL AND LEAVE THULE.

AT LAST THE DAWN, AND THE UNHAPPY GIRL PREPARES TO FACE THE TANGLE SHE HAS CREATED.

VAL GREETS HIS SHIVERING FIANCEE WITH BOISTEROUS GOOD-NATURE.

HE LAUGHS AND SINGS AS IF THE RAIN, THE MUD AND THE COLD ARE MUCH TO HIS LIKING, AS SHE BECOMES MORE MISERABLE HE GROWS MORE AND MORE CHEERFUL.

"WHAT A WONDERFUL ROMANCE OURS WILL BE; SIDE BY SIDE THROUGH SUN AND COLD WE WILL RIDE FROM ONE SPLENDID BATTLEFIELD TO ANOTHER— YOU SHALL COOK FOR ME, TEND MY WOUNDS AND EVERY DAY I WILL BRING YOU THE HEAD OF SOME CONQUERED FOE!" SHE SHUDDERS.

"IT GROWS DARK AND WE HAVE HAD NO MEAL THIS DAY—LET'S TAKE SHELTER IN YONDER CASTLE EVEN THOUGH I HAVE TO KILL ITS OWNER!" AND HE BURSTS OUT LAUGHING.

"WHAT A FOOL I AM," THINKS CLARIS, "TO GIVE UP THE LOVE OF TALL, CLUMSY ALFRED TO BE NURSEMAID TO THIS BLOODTHIRSTY GYPSY—OH! HOW I WISH THAT GATE WOULD FALL ON HIS HEAD!"

ALARIC THE GOTH 410 A.D.
SAVE THIS STAMP

"CLARIS, MEET THE NEW OWNER OF THE CASTLE," CRIES VAL ENTERING, AND WHO SHOULD HURRY FORWARD BUT ALFRED!

111 - 3-26-39

"WE HAVE HAD A WONDERFUL JOURNEY, ALFRED MY FRIEND, BUT SOMETHING TELLS ME CLARIS HAS CEASED TO THINK OF KINGS AND QUEENS AND WANTS ONLY...."
BUT ALFRED IS NO LONGER LISTENING, ONLY LOOKING DIVINELY HAPPY AND VERY, VERY FOOLISH AS MOST LOVERS DO.

NEXT WEEK: PEACE

CLOVIS 486 A.D. FIRST FRENCH KING
SAVE THIS STAMP

433 A.D.
THULE REGAINED
SAVE THIS STAMP

Prince Valiant

Registered U. S. Patent Office.

IN THE DAYS OF KING ARTHUR BY HAROLD R. FOSTER

ATTILA
THE WILD HUNS RAVAGE EUROPE
SAVE THIS STAMP

SYNOPSIS: THE FRIAR UTTERS A FEW WORDS AND CLARIS IS NO LONGER A MENACE TO THE THRONE AND ALFRED BECOMES A MARRIED MAN ··· CUPID HAS MADE A SIMPERING IDIOT OF THE BOISTEROUS, TALL ROGUE WHOSE RINGING LAUGH AND CLASHING SWORD HAD KEPT THULE BUSY.

VAL IS DISGUSTED — A GOOD FIGHTING MAN HAS BEEN SPOILED TO MAKE JUST ANOTHER HUSBAND.

VAL RIDES HOMEWARD THROUGH A SUNNY PEACEFUL LAND.

YES, A PEACEFUL LAND NOW ··· WHERE HEARTY YOUNG WARRIORS WEAR THEIR ARMOR ON A PEG.

FOR THE KING IS ALMOST TOO LENIENT FOR HIS TIMES AND ONLY ORDERS SUCH MURDERS AND EXECUTIONS AS ARE FOR THE PUBLIC GOOD, NEVER FOR PRIVATE PLEASURE — AND HIS PEOPLE GRUMBLE AT THE LACK OF ENTERTAINMENT.

EACH MORNING VAL TRAINS WITH THE OTHER KNIGHTS IN THE PALACE COURTYARD.

THE AFTERNOONS ARE SPENT MUCH AS HANDSOME PRINCES SPEND THEM EVERYWHERE.

VAL'S EVENINGS ARE MOST INTERESTING, SCHOLARS, POETS, TRAVELERS AND PHILOSOPHERS GATHER IN HIS ROOMS FOR DISCUSSION AND HE LEARNS MANY CURIOUS THINGS.

112 - 4 - 2 - 39

EVERY SATURDAY A GAY TOURNAMENT IS HELD AFTER WHICH THE SURVIVORS FEAST MERRILY.

HAL FOSTER

IN FACT, IT IS AN IDEAL KINGDOM WHERE JUSTICE, PROSPERITY AND PEACE REIGN — AND VAL IS BORED.

NEXT WEEK
KNIGHT ERRANT

ROME
SPQR
FEARS THE COMING OF ATTILA
SAVE THIS STAMP

412 A.D. ROMANS LEAVE BRITAIN
SAVE THIS STAMP

Prince Valiant

IN THE DAYS OF KING ARTHUR
BY HAROLD R. FOSTER

Registered U. S. Patent Office.

KING ARTHUR 420 TO 460 A.D.
SAVE THIS STAMP

SYNOPSIS: PEACE NOW REIGNS IN THULE AND THE MERCHANTS AND FARMERS ENJOY A PROSPERITY NOT OFTEN FOUND IN THESE ROUGH TIMES. THE WARRIORS ARE KEPT BUSY WITH FREQUENT TOURNAMENTS.

VAL PROFITS BY EVERY OPPORTUNITY TO IMPROVE HIS SKILL.

BUT HE LONGS FOR THOSE JOYOUS, TURBULENT DAYS UNDER KING ARTHUR.

SO HE GOES TO HIS FATHER AND TELLS HIM HE IS GOING TO SEEK ADVENTURE IN FAR COUNTRIES.

"YOU WILL DO NOTHING OF THE SORT," STORMS THE KING. "IT IS YOUR DUTY TO STAY HERE, LEARN STATECRAFT AND GOVERNMENT AND PREPARE YOURSELF FOR THE THRONE!"

"YES, FATHER — BUT YOU PREPARED YOURSELF IN QUITE ANOTHER WAY, FOR THEY STILL TELL OF YOUR BOISTEROUS YOUTH WHEN YOU BROKE LADIES' HEARTS AND MEN'S HEADS ALL ACROSS THE LAND."

"BUT MY FATHER WISHES ME TO STAY AT COURT AND BECOME A SMOOTH COURTIER AND A LOVELY DANCER—NOW JUST WHERE DID I LEAVE MY SEWING-BASKET?"

SO VAL STRAIGHTWAY GOES AND DOES JUST AS HE HAS PLANNED ALL ALONG....

113-4-9-39

....AND RIDES FROM THE CASTLE IN SEARCH OF ADVENTURE.

Copr. 1939, King Features Syndicate, Inc., World rights reserved

THE KING WATCHES HIS IMPUDENT, HEADSTRONG SON RIDE AWAY—JUST AS HE, HIMSELF, HAD DONE SO MANY YEARS AGO.

NEXT WEEK KNIGHT ERRANTRY

HAL FOSTER

KING ARTHUR'S DRAGON CREST — SAVE THIS STAMP

Prince Valiant

IN THE DAYS OF KING ARTHUR
BY HAROLD R FOSTER

Registered U. S. Patent Office.

TRISTRAM — SAVE THIS STAMP

SYNOPSIS – SO PRINCE VALIANT DEFIES HIS FATHER, BECOMES KNIGHT ERRANT AND GOES GAILY ADVENTURING, AND AFTER HIS LEAVING, THE NOISY COURT BECOMES QUIET, VERY QUIET.

"IT SEEMS", SAYS THE OBSERVANT KING, *"THAT I AM NOT THE ONLY ONE WHO MISSES THE IMPUDENT RASCAL."*

MEANWHILE, VAL IS WANDERING HAPPILY AFIELD, READY FOR ANY ADVENTURE THAT MIGHT TURN UP.

A WANDERER'S HARDSHIPS ARE MANY, BUT HE ENJOYS THE FREEDOM.

ONE DAY VAL CHANCES UPON THE WORK OF BRUTAL ROBBERS — FILLED WITH RAGE HE GIVES CHASE.....

..... AND OVERTAKES THEM IN A FOREST GLADE

LATER, WHILE WIPING OFF HIS SWORD, HE NOTICES FOR THE FIRST TIME THAT A STORM APPROACHES.

THE CAVE OF TIME

..... AND SO SEEKS SHELTER IN A NEARBY CAVE.

114 – 4 -16 -39

Copr. 1939, King Features Syndicate, Inc., World rights reserved.

HE IS PREPARING TO SPEND THE NIGHT WITHIN THIS SHELTER WHEN HE IS STARTLED BY AN OMINOUS COUGH. TURNING HE FINDS HE IS NOT ALONE....

NEXT WEEK *The* WITCH WOMAN

LAUNCELOT DU LAKE — SAVE THIS STAMP

Prince Valiant

IN THE DAYS OF KING ARTHUR
BY HAROLD R. FOSTER

SIR MODRED — SAVE THIS STAMP

Registered U. S. Patent Office

SYNOPSIS—VAL TAKES REFUGE FROM A STORM IN WHAT HE BELIEVES IS AN EMPTY CAVE, HEARING A SLIGHT COUGH HE TURNS, STARTLED, TO FIND A STRANGE WOMAN STANDING BEHIND HIM.

"PARDON, LADY, DO I TRESPASS?"

"NO, LAD, FOR SOONER OR LATER ALL THINGS MUST COME AT LAST TO THIS FORLORN PLACE," ANSWERED THE WITCH-WOMAN. "SHALL WE DINE?"

"I DO NOT UNDERSTAND THE MEANING OF YOUR WORDS, BUT YOUR WINE IS POTENT. ALREADY MY HEAD SWIMS."

"THIS CAVE IS THE TROPHY-ROOM OF 'TIME' WHICH NO ONE DARE ENTER."

"I'LL DARE ANY ADVENTURE!" AND DRAWING THE 'SINGING SWORD', VAL ENTERS THE SILENT GLOOM.

A BLUE AND SINISTER GLOW ILLUMINATES THIS MISCHANCY PLACE. IN A FAR CORNER THE BENT FIGURE OF AN AGED MAN CAN BE DIMLY SEEN.

HORSA — SAVE THIS STAMP

"WHO ARE YOU?" FALTERS THE SCARED YOUTH. "I AM THE ULTIMATE CONQUEROR OF ALL THINGS AND MY TROPHIES ARE THE ALTARS OF FORGOTTEN GODS, THE THRONES OF KINGS, SPLENDID CITIES AND FORTRESSES UNCONQUERABLE."

"NONE MAY WITHSTAND 'TIME'.... I VANQUISH THEM ALL IN THE END.... WOULD YOU CARE TO WRESTLE WITH ME?"

NEXT WEEK: THE CONTEST

PALAMIDES

JOYOUSE GARDE
LAUNCELOT
SAVE THIS STAMP

Prince Valiant

IN THE DAYS OF
KING ARTHUR
BY
HAROLD R. FOSTER

Registered U. S. Patent Office.

CAMELOT
THE ROYAL PALACE
SAVE THIS STAMP

SYNOPSIS: IN THE SHELTER OF A GREAT CAVE VAL MEETS A WITCH-WOMAN WHO GIVES HIM A POTENT DRINK AND A GRIM WARNING, WHICH HE IGNORES AND ENTERS THE ABODE OF "TIME"

"YOU DON'T BELIEVE THAT 'TIME' IS UNCONQUERABLE... THEN SHALL WE WRESTLE?"

THE STALWART YOUTH PICKS UP THE SENILE OLD MAN TO FLING HIM AMONG HIS DUSTY TROPHIES.

BUT THE ANCIENT CREATURE CLINGS TENACIOUSLY WITH WEAK, FRAIL HANDS, AS VAL STRIVES TO FREE HIMSELF.

HOW LONG THEY STRUGGLED IN THAT WEIRD, DIM PLACE VAL COULD NEVER AFTERWARDS TELL, BUT HE GROWS WEARY... WEARY....

WITH A CACKLING LAUGH "TIME" HURLS HIS SKINNY ADVERSARY AMONG THE WORLD'S DISCARDED TOYS.

AS VAL STUMBLES OUT OF THAT FANTASTIC CAVERN HE HEARS A THIN, CRACKED VOICE GLOATING, "ALL CONTEND WITH 'TIME' AND ALL ARE VANQUISHED."

SAVE THIS STAMP
DOLOROUS GARDE
MORGAN LE FEY

AT THE CAVE'S MOUTH THE WITCH-WOMAN CALMLY WAITS THE RETURN OF ALL THAT REMAINS OF A PROUD PRINCE.

"YOU MUST BE TIRED, GRANDFATHER, SIT DOWN AND REFRESH YOURSELF."

116   4-30-39

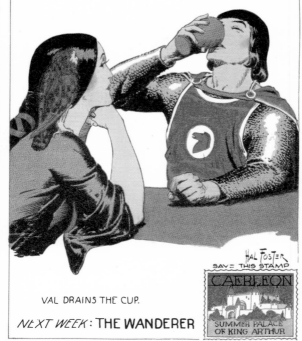

VAL DRAINS THE CUP.

NEXT WEEK: THE WANDERER

HAL FOSTER
SAVE THIS STAMP
CAERLEON
SUMMER PALACE
OF KING ARTHUR

Registered U. S. Patent Office.

SYNOPSIS: THE WITCH-WOMAN GIVES VAL A POTENT DRINK AND A WARNING WHICH HE IGNORES. ENTERING THE CAVE HE WRESTLES WITH **TIME** AND IS VANQUISHED.

"DRINK AND BE REFRESHED POOR, RECKLESS FOOL." THE WEARY OLD PRINCE GRASPS THE GOBLET.

"AH! HOW STIMULATING IS THE WINE," SAYS VAL, LOWERING THE CUP.

THEN TERROR SEIZES HIM AND HE FLEES *"TIS A HORRIBLE TRICK. NO SUCH THING COULD POSSIBLY HAVE HAPPENED!"*

"HOW TERRIBLE TO BE OLD AND WEAK AND HOW GOOD IT IS TO BE YOUNG AND STRONG AGAIN — I MUST REMEMBER THAT."

HE RIDES FAR AND COMES TO THE SEA OVER WHICH A GREAT STORM IS APPROACHING.

LIGHTS SHINING THROUGH THE STORM PROMISE SHELTER.

HE FINDS A TAVERN FREQUENTED BY SAILORS AND TRAVELERS FROM FAR, STRANGE LANDS.

117-5-7-39

AS THE STORM WITHOUT RAGES, WEIRD TALES ARE TOLD OF FABULOUS ISLES AND WONDROUS WALLED CITIES.

Copr. 1939, King Features Syndicate, Inc., World rights reserved

AND ALL THIS WHILE A HAGGARD WANDERER IS NEARING THE TAVERN WITH ASTOUNDING NEWS.
NEXT WEEK
"ROME HAS FALLEN!"

HAL FOSTER

Prince Valiant

IN THE DAYS OF KING ARTHUR

BY HAROLD R FOSTER

GRIFFON — SAVE THIS STAMP

UNICORN — SAVE THIS STAMP

Registered U. S. Patent Office.

SYNOPSIS: WHILE RIDING AT ADVENTURE AS KNIGHT ERRANT, VAL HAS STRANGE EXPERIENCES. TO-NIGHT HE SHELTERS FROM THE STORM IN A TAVERN AND HEARS WONDROUS TALES OF FAR, STRANGE LANDS.

THERE COMES A POUNDING AT THE DOOR AND IN FROM THE STORM COMES A BATTERED WANDERER.

"ROME HAS FALLEN TO ATTILA AND TO THE SOUTH ALL EUROPE IS IN FLAMES, AS THE HUNS RAVAGE AND KILL."

"BUT ANDELKRAG STILL STANDS; UP ABOVE THE SMOKE AND FLAMES SOAR THE TOWERS OF ANDELKRAG, THE UNCONQUERABLE."

VAL DRAWS THE HAGGARD WANDERER TO A SEAT BESIDE HIM — "TELL ME OF THIS UNCONQUERABLE FORTRESS"

"TO THE FORTRESS OF ANDELKRAG, PRINCE CAMERON OF-THE-HIGH-HEAD GATHERS ALL WHO LOVE BEAUTY, MUSIC, POETRY AND NOBLE DEEDS. OFTEN HAS HE BEEN ASSAILED, BUT WHEN HIS LAUGHING WARRIORS MAN THE BATTLEMENT VICTORY IS THEIRS....TROUBADORS EVERYWHERE SING OF CAMERON'S DEEDS.... NOW ONLY ANDELKRAG STANDS ABOVE THE SMOKE OF BURNING EUROPE."

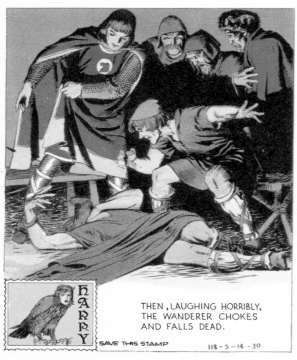

THEN, LAUGHING HORRIBLY, THE WANDERER CHOKES AND FALLS DEAD.

HARRY — SAVE THIS STAMP

118-5-14-39

"THE RED PLAGUE"! WHISPERS A SEAMAN AND ALL RUSH OUT INTO THE NIGHT

THE INN-KEEPER SETS FIRE TO THE TAVERN AND ALL HIS POSSESSIONS. THEN HE, TOO, TAKES FLIGHT AND DISAPPEARS IN THE HOWLING DARKNESS.

NEXT WEEK —"FLIGHT"

HAL FOSTER

SAVE THIS STAMP

DRAGON

Prince Valiant

Registered U. S. Patent Office.

HELMET 1 FIRST A CAP OF PADDED WOOL · SAVE THIS STAMP

HELMET 2 CHAIN MAIL OVER THE CAP · SAVE THIS STAMP

Synopsis: FROM A DYING WANDERER VAL HEARS A RUMOR OF THE FALL OF ROME AND THE RAVAGE OF ALL EUROPE BY ATTILA AND HIS HUNS —ONLY BRAVE CAMORAN IN HIS CASTLE ANDELKRAG HOLDS OUT AGAINST THE SAVAGE

"WHAT COULD BE MORE SPLENDID THAN TO FIGHT SIDE BY SIDE WITH GALLANT CAMORAN!" AND VAL TURNS TO THE SOUTHEAST.

LEAVING HIS FATHER'S KINGDOM HE RIDES MANY DAYS UNTIL FLEEING REFUGEES AND THE SMOKE OF BURNING VILLAGES GIVE WARNING OF THE HUNS' PRESENCE

NEVER HAS EUROPE BEEN MORE TERRIBLY VISITED VAL SUFFERS SEVERELY FROM THE LACK OF FOOD.

ONCE A BAND OF WANDERING HUNS SWEEPS DOWN ON THE YOUNG KNIGHT AND THERE IS NO ESCAPE.

HIS HEAVIER ARMOR SAVES HIM FROM SERIOUS HURT AND HIS FOES MELT AWAY BEFORE THE FLAMING CIRCLE OF THE "SINGING SWORD."

CUTTING A PLENTIFUL SUPPLY OF HORSE MEAT VAL LEAVES THE DANGEROUS PLAINS AND FINDS A WAY THROUGH THE MOUNTAINS.

FROM A REFUGEE HE LEARNS THAT EMPEROR VALENTINIAN HAS PURCHASED A SHAMEFUL PEACE FOR ROME BY GIVING HIS SISTER AS WIFE TO BRUTAL ATTILA.

HELMET 3 FOR WAR · SAVE THIS STAMP

119 – 5 – 21 – 39

PRINCE VAL SHARES HIS FOOD AND THE GRATEFUL MAN GUIDES HIM ACROSS A HAZARDOUS PASS.

Copr. 1939, King Features Syndicate, Inc., World rights reserved.

AND THERE, BELOW THEM, IS ANDELKRAG, ITS TOWERS RISING ABOVE THE SMOKE AND TURMOIL OF BATTLE.

NEXT WEEK "THROUGH THE LINES"

HAL FOSTER

HELMET 4 FOR TOURNAMENTS · SAVE THIS STAMP

THE GUIDE
SAVE THIS STAMP

Prince Valiant

IN THE DAYS OF KING ARTHUR
BY
HAROLD R. FOSTER

Registered U. S. Patent Office.

ATTILA
SAVE THIS STAMP

PRINCE VALIANT HAS RIDDEN FAR AND DANGEROUSLY TO COME AT LAST TO ANDELKRAG. AND NOW BELOW HIM STANDS CAMORAN'S FAR-FAMED FORTRESS SURROUNDED BY THE INVADING HUNS. HOW CAN HE ALONE ENTER A CASTLE THAT HAS FOR MONTHS DEFIED THE MIGHT OF ATTILA?

LONG HE STUDIES BEFORE A PLAN IS FORMED. THEN GIVING HIS BELOVED WAR-HORSE INTO THE KEEPING OF HIS GUIDE, HE STRIDES DOWN THE SLOPE.

CIRCLING THE ENEMY CAMP IN THE DARKNESS, VAL ENTERS THE RIVER THAT FILLS THE CASTLE MOAT.

HE HAS ALMOST REACHED THE MOAT WHEN HIS WAY IS BARRED BY A RAFT PILED HIGH WITH FUEL.

IT IS A FIRE-RAFT WITH WHICH, ON THE MORROW, THE HUNS HOPE TO BURN AWAY THE DRAW-BRIDGE AND GATE OF ANDELKRAG. WITH FLINT AND STEEL ......

... VAL DESTROYS THEIR WORK. "TREACHERY", THEY CRY AND SEARCH FIERCELY FOR THE CULPRIT!

NEXT WEEK:
CAMORAN

HAL FOSTER
SAVE THIS STAMP
ATTILA'S
ROMAN BRIDE

Synopsis: FINDING A FIRE RAFT WITH WHICH THE HUNS HOPE TO BURN AWAY THE OAKEN GATES OF ANDELKRAG, VAL SETS IT ALIGHT.

THE ANGRY HUNS COME RUNNING TO FIND THE CULPRIT.

CROUCHED NEAR THE BANK VAL COVERS HIMSELF WITH MUD AS THE SEARCH COMES CLOSER.

SUDDENLY THE DRAW-BRIDGE COMES DOWN WITH A CLANG AND CAMORAN AND HIS WARRIORS DASH FORTH, SHOUTING.

INTO THE CONFUSED HUNS THEY SWEEP LIKE A SCYTHE AMONG WHEAT.

SWIFTLY VAL WADES TO THE BRIDGE AND HAILS THE GUARD. *"I AM PRINCE VALIANT, KNIGHT OF THE ROUND TABLE COME TO JOIN YOUR RANKS."*

THAT HE IS INDEED EVERY INCH A PRINCE NO MAN CAN DOUBT!

THEN CAMORAN RETURNS WITH HIS MEN, LAUGHING AT THE CONFUSION OF THE ENEMY.

"HELLO, YOUNGSTER," HE GRINS. *"FIGHT HARD, SING MERRILY AND YOU WILL BE WELCOME."*

HAL FOSTER

"TO OUR NEW COMPANION — MAY HE CARVE A NAME FOR HIMSELF WITH THAT GREAT SHINING SWORD."

NEXT WEEK: **THE DAY'S WORK**

VAL OF THE FENS
SAVE THIS STAMP

Prince Valiant

IN THE DAYS OF KING ARTHUR
BY HAROLD R FOSTER

Registered U. S. Patent Office.

VAL THE SQUIRE
SAVE THIS STAMP

Synopsis: VAL SLIPS THROUGH THE HORDES OF BESIEGING HUNS AND JOINS THE GALLANT DEFENDERS OF ANDELKRAG UNDER THEIR PRINCE, BRAVE CAMORAN.

AT DAWN THE NIGHT-WATCH DESCENDS AND THE WARRIORS MAN THE BATTLEMENTS.

...AND THEY GO INTO THE FRAY, SINGING THEIR BATTLE CHANTS AND LAUGHING AS THEY FIGHT

NOTHING SEEMS TO DAMPEN THE HIGH SPIRITS OF THESE COURAGEOUS PEOPLE.

THE HUNS ARE LIKE DEMONS IN THEIR FURIOUS ATTACK AND THE WEEKS GO BY LIKE A LONG NIGHTMARE.

HAL FOSTER

SIR VALIANT
SAVE THIS STAMP

122 6-11-39

EVER IN THE FOREFRONT IS CAMORAN, AN EXAMPLE TO ALL IN THE SPLENDOR OF HIS YOUTH.

...AND WHEN NIGHT SILENCES THE ATTACK, THE DAY'S SURVIVORS DINE NOBLY WITH SONG AND GAY MUSIC.

NEXT WEEK— "THE BATTLE"

VAL PRINCE OF THULE
SAVE THIS STAMP

Prince Valiant

IN THE DAYS OF KING ARTHUR
BY HAROLD R FOSTER

Registered U. S. Patent Office.

Synopsis: ATTILA AND HIS ROMAN BRIDE RETIRE INTO PANNONIA, WHICH IS NOW KNOWN AS HUNGARY, BUT HIS FOLLOWERS SWARM IN UNCOUNTED NUMBERS ABOUT UNCONQUERABLE ANDELKRAG.

THE TIRELESS HUNS DIVERT THE RIVER AND DRY UP THE CASTLE MOAT.

WITH THE MOAT FILLED IN, HUGE SIEGE TOWERS LURCH PONDEROUSLY FORWARD.

BUT THE DEFENDERS ROCK THEM BACK AND FORTH WITH GRAPPLES UNTIL THEY FALL CRASHING TO EARTH.

THEN HUGE PROTECTED BATTERING RAMS ARE MOVED AGAINST THE WALLS.

DAY AND NIGHT IS HEARD THE STEADY THUD OF THE RAMS UNTIL AT LAST THE WALL CRUMBLES.

THE HUNS RUSH THROUGH ONLY TO FIND AN INNER WALL BUILT AROUND THE WEAK PLACE.

WELL-PLANNED SORTIES THRUST OUT LIKE A SWORD INTO THE HUN'S CAMP, BURNING AND DESTROYING AND RETURNING AS SWIFTLY AS THEY CAME.

123 – 6 – 18 – 39

VAL WONDERS HOW LONG THE LAVISH BANQUETS CAN LAST, FOR THE HUNS' RESOURCES ARE UNLIMITED.

"WOULD IT NOT BE WELL TO CONSERVE OUR SUPPLIES, CAMORAN?" "SIR VALIANT, NO ENEMY WILL EVER ALTER THE WAYS OF LIVING AT ANDELKRAG. WE WILL LIVE, LOVE, FIGHT AND DIE LIKE GENTLEMEN!"

NEXT WEEK– "THE LAST BANQUET"

THE LUTE

SAVE THIS STAMP

THE DUDELSACK

SAVE THIS STAMP

Synopsis: THOUGH ASSAILED FURIOUSLY BY ATTILA'S UNTOLD THOUSANDS, ANDELKRAG STILL STANDS UNCONQUERED. THE SCARRED WARRIORS ON THE BATTLEMENTS ARE FEWER NOW, BUT UNDAUNTED, AS THE WEEKS DRAG INTO MONTHS.

IN THE LULL BETWEEN ATTACKS CONTESTS ARE HELD AT THE EXPENSE OF THE HUNS.

WITHIN THE FORTRESS LIFE GOES ON GAILY AS EVER.

BUT UPON THE CRUMBLING WALLS IS ETERNAL VIGILANCE.

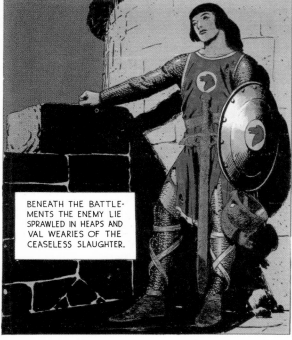

BENEATH THE BATTLEMENTS THE ENEMY LIE SPRAWLED IN HEAPS AND VAL WEARIES OF THE CEASELESS SLAUGHTER.

THE SACKBUT

THE FAGOT

SAVE THIS STAMP

124 : 6-25-39

THAT DREADED DAY AT LAST ARRIVES - OF FOOD AND DRINK THERE IS NO MORE!

THEN CAMORAN ARISES SMILING. "THE BARBARIANS RULE FROM SEA TO SEA - WE ARE THE LAST OF THE WARRIOR-TROUBADORS. BECAUSE OF US THE WORLD HAS BEEN A BETTER PLACE TO LIVE IN, BUT NOW OUR FOOD IS GONE SO TO-MORROW WE WILL DO THAT WHICH WE HAVE TO DO."

HAL FOSTER

NEXT WEEK: "THE LAST MARCH"

MEDIEVAL GUITAR

SAVE THIS STAMP

SWORD FROM FAR CATHAY — SAVE THIS STAMP

Prince Valiant

IN THE DAYS OF KING ARTHUR
By HAROLD R. FOSTER

Registered U.S. Patent Office.

ROMAN SHORT SWORD — SAVE THIS STAMP

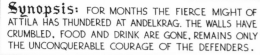

Synopsis: FOR MONTHS THE FIERCE MIGHT OF ATTILA HAS THUNDERED AT ANDELKRAG. THE WALLS HAVE CRUMBLED, FOOD AND DRINK ARE GONE, REMAINS ONLY THE UNCONQUERABLE COURAGE OF THE DEFENDERS.

AT DAWN ALL THE VAST TREASURE IS CARRIED INTO THE LOFTY HALL.

AND PLACED IN A DEEP VAULT BENEATH THE FLOOR.

AND ONE BY ONE THE GRACEFUL, HIGH-SPIRITED LADIES MOUNT SLOWLY THE TOWER STAIRWAY.

CAMORAN, HIMSELF, APPLIES THE TORCH THAT WILL BRING ROOF AND WALLS CRASHING DOWN.

"THE LADIES, CAMORAN, THEY NEVER DESCENDED FROM THE TOWER." AND THE FACE OF CAMORAN IS TERRIBLE TO SEE AS HE ANSWERS —

"THE LADIES DO NOT CHOOSE TO FALL INTO THE HANDS OF THOSE WHO WAIT OUTSIDE."

VAL LOOKS THROUGH THE LOOP-HOLE INTO THE FACES OF THE WILD HUNS AND UNDERSTANDS.

125: 7-2-39

HAL FOSTER

QUIETLY, CALMLY THE LAST OF THE WARRIOR-TROUBADOURS GO TO MEET THEIR FOE AND FEARFUL IS THE GLEAM OF THEIR EYES.

NEXT WEEK: "HOW HEROES DIE"

CAMORAN
SAVE THIS STAMP

JESTER
SAVE THIS STAMP

Synopsis: BEHIND THE BATTERED WALLS OF THE UNCONQUERABLE ANDELKRAG, THE GALLANT DEFENDERS FACE FAMINE . THEY CHOOSE TO MEET DEATH AS WARRIORS FIGHTING THE ENEMY RATHER THAN STARVE MISERABLY. THE FORTRESS IS SET ABLAZE.

DOWN A SECRET PASSAGE BENEATH THE MOAT CAMORAN LEADS THE REMNANT OF THE WARRIOR-TROUBADOURS.

THE TUNNEL'S END IS BLOCKED BY A GREAT ROCK, BUT THEY HURL THEIR WEIGHT AGAINST IT AND IT YIELDS.

OUT INTO THE AFTERNOON SUNLIGHT THEY LEAP, SHOUTING THEIR BATTLE-CRY.

THE BARBARIANS TURN TO MEET THE CHARGING, MAIL-CLAD HURRICANE.

THROUGH THE SCREAMING MASS THE MEN OF ANDELKRAG CUT A FEARFUL CRIMSON ROAD – THEN WHEEL ABOUT AND RETURN – FEWER NOW, BUT STILL UNDAUNTED.

THE SUN GOES DOWN AND STILL A HEROIC FEW FIGHT ON IN THE GATHERING DUSK.

Hal Foster

SIR KERIN
SAVE THIS STAMP

AT LAST ONLY SIR VALIANT STANDS, ALONE WITHIN THE FLAMING CIRCLE OF THE FEARFUL "SINGING SWORD."

Copr. 1939 King Features Syndicate, Inc.
World rights reserved   126: 7-9-39

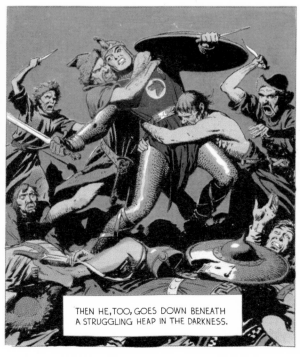

THEN HE, TOO, GOES DOWN BENEATH A STRUGGLING HEAP IN THE DARKNESS.

LONG AND DESPERATELY THEY STRUGGLE, THEN SLOWLY ONE STAGGERS TO HIS FEET, ALONE, ON A FIELD LIT ONLY BY BLAZING ANDELKRAG!

NEXT WEEK "CAMORAN'S BIER"

YOUNG ARAINE
SAVE THIS STAMP

MYSTERIOUS DEATH OF ATTILA
SAVE THIS STAMP

Prince Valiant

IN THE DAYS OF KING ARTHUR
BY HAROLD R. FOSTER

HUNS GATHER IN HUNGARY
SAVE THIS STAMP

Registered U. S. Patent Office

Synopsis: WHEN DEATH APPROACHES THE MEN OF ANDELKRAG MARCH OUT FROM THEIR BURNING FORTRESS AND MEET IT LIKE WARRIORS. NIGHT HAS FALLEN ERE THE LAST HERO FALLS.

BUT THAT LAST WARRIOR RISES AGAIN TO FIND HIS ENEMIES HAVE MELTED AWAY INTO THE DARKNESS-- FROM THEIR CAMP COMES A MOURNFUL WAILING —

"ATTILA IS DEAD, ATTILA IS DEAD." AND THEY GO STREAMING AWAY OVER THE PASS THAT LEADS INTO HUNGARY (WHERE QUARRELS AMONG THE LEADERS FINALLY BREAK THE POWER OF THE HUNS).

A LINE OF CONQUERED FOES LEADS TO THE SPOT WHERE CAMORAN HAD MADE HIS LAST STAND.

VAL TAKES HIS GALLANT CAPTAIN IN HIS ARMS AND STAGGERS TO THE TUNNEL'S MOUTH

UNDER THE MOAT AND WEARILY, STEP BY STEP UP THE EASTERN TOWER.

"ALL ANDELKRAG SHALL BE YOUR BIER." AND WRAPPED IN A PURPLE BANNER VAL GIVES HIS CHIEFTIAN TO THE FLAMES.

HIGH UP ON THE HILLSIDE AWAY FROM THE HUN-INFESTED PASS, VAL TURNS TO WATCH THE CASTLE WALLS COME CRASHING DOWN.

127: 7-16-39

THEN SLEEPS UNTIL THE NEXT DAY'S NOON....

Copr. 1939, King Features Syndicate, Inc., World rights reserved

HAL FOSTER

....WHILE TWO SHREWD, AVARICIOUS EYES PEER HUNGRILY AT THE JEWELS SPARKLING ON THE HILT OF THE "SINGING SWORD."

NEXT WEEK: "SLITH-"

Prince Valiant

IN THE DAYS OF KING ARTHUR
BY
HAROLD R. FOSTER

Registered U. S. Patent Office.

Synopsis: ANDELKRAG, THE UNCONQUERABLE, BECOMES A SMOLDERING RUIN AND THE ONE BATTERED SURVIVOR STAGGERS WEARILY INTO THE HILLS. WHEN HE AWAKES THE NOON DAY SUN IS SPARKLING ON THE JEWELED HILT OF HIS "SINGING SWORD."

WHILE ACROSS THE POOL TWO SHREWD EYES ARE PEERING HUNGRILY AT THE FLASHING GEMS WAITING.

VAL STEPS TO THE EDGE OF THE CLEAR SPRING AND REMOVES HIS SWORD AND MAIL.

THE COOL, SPARKLING WATER FEELS SO GOOD ON HIS BRUISED AND WEARY BODY THAT HE FAILS TO NOTICE THE CROUCHING FIGURE CREEPING CLOSER.

UNTIL A DISLODGED PEBBLE COMES RATTLING DOWN AND SPLASHES BESIDE HIM.

THEN COMES ACTION SO QUICK THAT HIS ATTACKER NEVER KNEW WHAT HAD HAPPENED UNTIL ········

····HE FINDS HIMSELF HELPLESS. VAL IS CALMLY DROWNING HIM WHEN CURIOSITY GETS THE BETTER OF HIM AND THE VICTIM IS HAULED OUT ON THE BANK.

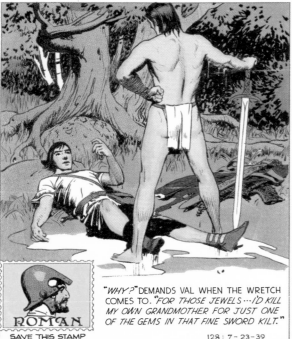

"WHY?" DEMANDS VAL WHEN THE WRETCH COMES TO. "FOR THOSE JEWELS ··· I'D KILL MY OWN GRANDMOTHER FOR JUST ONE OF THE GEMS IN THAT FINE SWORD KILT."

128 : 7-23-39

"FOR I AM SLITH, THIEF AND ROBBER, JUGGLER, ACTOR, SINGER AND MAGICIAN. I LIVE BY MY WITS AND EVERY MAN IS MY ENEMY. I AM REALLY NOT WORTH KILLING ··· I HOPE," AND GRINS DISARMINGLY.

HAL FOSTER

VAL LAUGHS AT HIS IMPUDENCE AND KICKS HIM TO HIS FEET—WHEREUPON THE GRATEFUL RASCAL LEADS THE WAY TO HIS NEARBY CAMP AND A WELCOME SUPPER.

NEXT WEEK: "BAD COMPANY"

Synopsis: PRINCE VALIANT SAVES THE LIFE OF SLITH SIMPLY BY NOT KILLING THE GRINNING RASCAL, EVEN THOUGH HE DESERVES IT ····· IN GRATITUDE HE PLAYS HOST·····ON SILVER PLATTERS, TOO.

"WON THEM WITH CROOKED DICE," SLITH EXPLAINS, "FROM A NOBLEMAN WHO OVERTAXED HIS SERFS ····· ONE OF US WAS A VILLAIN."

"I WAS STOLEN WHEN A CHILD, SOLD INTO SLAVERY. I'VE BEEN BEATEN, ROBBED AND HUNTED LIKE A WILD BEAST – I AM WHAT MEN HAVE MADE ME."

"SO I EARN MY BREAD BY TRICKS AND TRICKERY. I ENTERTAIN FOR FOOD, GAMBLE FOR PLEASURE AND CHEAT FOR PROFIT."

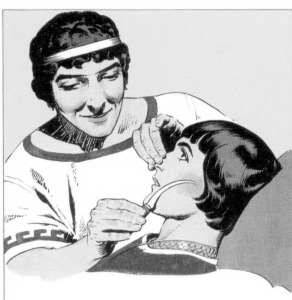

"THESE MOUNTAINS ARE FULL OF REFUGEES AND BANDITS – HOLD STILL!···AND ON THE PLAINS ARE BANDS OF HUNS."

"WE NEED FOOD SO WE WILL FIND A CAMP AND I'LL SHOW YOU HOW I GET A LIVING."

"LOOK! A BAND OF HUNS APPROACHES– YOU HIDE AND I'LL TRICK THE STUPIDS INTO FEEDING US."

HIDDEN AMONG THE ROCKS, VAL WATCHES SLITH DELUDING THE HATED HUNS.

129 : 7 - 30 - 39

OH! HOW HE HATES THE HUNS!··· THE HUNS WHO HAD DESTROYED GLORIOUS ANDELKRAG AND ALL ITS SPLENDID PEOPLE ····· HE STANDS UP, SCOWLING.

THE SUN, FLASHING ON THE JEWELED SWORD HILT CATCHES THE HUNS' EYES.

NEXT WEEK: **AGAIN THE SWORD SINGS"**

Prince Valiant

FUR, LEATHER, WOOL
SAVE THIS STAMP

TARTARY
FELT, WOOL
SAVE THIS STAMP

Synopsis: SIR VALIANT'S FIERCE PRIDE WILL NOT ALLOW HIM TO HIDE FROM THE DESPISED HUNS, WHILE SLITH CUNNINGLY TRICKS THEM OUT OF A FOOD SUPPLY ····· SO HE REVEALS HIMSELF, HIS JEWELED SWORD HILT ALL SHINING IN THE SUNLIGHT.

"PLUNDER", CRY THE BARBARIANS AND COME SWARMING UP THE HILLSIDE.

SLITH FITS A MISSILE IN HIS SLING AND IS ABOUT TO CRACK A SKULL OR TWO, WHEN HIS ATTENTION IS ARRESTED ·····

···ARRESTED BY VAL'S QUIET, CONFIDENT MANNER, AS WITH NEITHER SHIELD NOR HELMET HE AWAITS THE ONSLAUGHT OF THE CLIMBING HUNS. SLITH SEEKS A VANTAGE POINT, TO WATCH, HIS SLING READY.

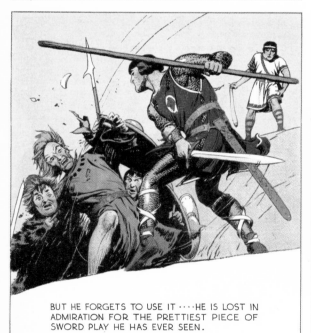

BUT HE FORGETS TO USE IT ····HE IS LOST IN ADMIRATION FOR THE PRETTIEST PIECE OF SWORD PLAY HE HAS EVER SEEN.

FOR VAL SEEMS TO KNOW EVERY MOVE HIS ENEMIES ARE ABOUT TO MAKE AND HIS NIMBLE SWORD FLASHES OUT UNEXPECTEDLY.

WITH HIS STAFF HE SMOTHERS THEIR ATTACK, MANEUVERING SO THEY ARE ALWAYS IN EACH OTHER'S WAY.

WHEN THE LAST HUN SUDDENLY REMEMBERS HEALTHIER PLACES FAR AWAY, SLITH IS APPLAUDING JOYOUSLY.

SOUTH EUROPE
WOOL, SAMITE
SAVE THIS STAMP

130: 8-6-39

"I KNOW YOUR SECRET", HE CRIES, "CO-ORDINATION! SO QUICK IS YOUR EYE YOU SEE THINGS PRACTICALLY IN SLOW MOTION ···THE CHARM OF THE 'SINGING SWORD' HAS NOTHING TO DO WITH IT."

Copr. 1939, King Features Syndicate, Inc., World rights reserved.

HAL FOSTER

"LISTEN, WORM! THE SINGING SWORD BEARS A CHARM FOR HIM WHO USES IT IN A GOOD CAUSE. I PREFER TO BELIEVE THAT!"

NEXT WEEK: "SETTING A TRAP"

CATHAY
SILK, BROCADE
SAVE THIS STAMP

GALAHAD
SAVE THIS STAMP

Prince Valiant

Registered U. S. Patent Office.

IN THE DAYS OF
KING ARTHUR
BY
HAROLD R. FOSTER

SAW THE HOLY GRAIL
PERCIVAL
SAVE THIS STAMP

Synopsis: VAL CONDUCTS A CLASS IN SWORDSMANSHIP— THREE HUNS FAIL TO MAKE THE GRADE, BUT THE FOURTH LEARNS HIS LESSON JUST IN TIME—AND ESCAPES.

"SIR VALIANT, YOU WILL HAVE TO CONCEAL THAT JEWELED SWORD-HILT AND SCABBARD—ELSE EVERY BRIGAND AND HUN IN THESE INFESTED MOUNTAINS WILL TRY TO MURDER YOU FOR THEM."

"INCLUDING YOURSELF, SLITH, MY NIMBLE FRIEND······ WELL, LET'S SEE WHAT THE LATE HUNS HAVE LEFT US IN THE WAY OF FOOD AND CLOTHING."

SEEING THE VALUE OF SLITH'S ADVICE, VAL MAKES A COVER FOR THE JEWELED SCABBARD AND PUTS A BINDING OVER THE BRIGHT HILT.

"NOW THIS COSTUME MAY SUIT YOU, BUT NOT ME. I NOT ONLY LOOK LIKE A HUN, BUT, BY ZEUS, I SMELL LIKE ONE!"

FOLLOWED BY THE PROTESTING SLITH, VAL GOES IN SEARCH OF A COSTUME FITTING HIS RANK··· AND HIS VANITY!

HIGH ABOVE THE PASS WHEREBY THE PLUNDERING HUNS RETURN INTO PANNONIA THE TWO LADS WATCH FOR VAL'S NEW SUIT TO COME ALONG.

JUST AT SUNDOWN VAL EXCLAIMS:— "LOOK··· LEADING THAT TROOP IS MY NEW OUTFIT WITH AN UNFORTUNATE HUN CHIEFTAIN IN IT!"

131- 8-13-39

WHILE THE HUNS ARE CAMPING FOR THE NIGHT, VAL PREPARES A TRICK THAT WILL SEPARATE THE UNLUCKY LEADER FROM HIS FOLLOWERS.

HAL FOSTER

AT DAWN THEY ARE IN THEIR PLACE PREPARED TO TAKE A SUIT OF CLOTHING AWAY FROM A TROOP OF FIFTY ARMED HUNS.

NEXT WEEK "SLITH ABANDONED"

Synopsis: VAL FINDS HIS BATTERED NORTHERN ARMOR UNSUITED TO SOUTHERN EUROPE. HE GOES SHOPPING FOR A NEW OUTFIT AND, WHEN HE SEES IT, FINDS HE HAS TO REMOVE THE HUN INSIDE. AT A STEEP POINT ON THE TRAIL VAL PREPARES A TRAP TO SEPARATE HIS VICTIM FROM THE FOLLOWING TROOP OF RAIDERS.

AS THE HUN CAPTAIN PASSES THEIR HIDING-PLACE, VAL FORCES OUT THE TRIGGER AND THE GREAT PINE COMES CRASHING DOWN···

····THERE IS A GREAT CONFUSION AS THE TERRIFIED HORSES REAR AND PLUNGE···VAL SPRINGS FORWARD···

··· BUT HIS CHOSEN VICTIM IS BEING CARRIED DOWN THE TRAIL ON HIS TERROR-STRICKEN MOUNT·····VAL LEAPS UPON THE SECOND HUN.

A SHORT, DEADLY STRUGGLE AND VAL IS CLATTERING RECKLESSLY DOWN THE STEEP, ROCKY PATH IN PURSUITE.

CLOSE ON THE HUN'S LEFT FLANK RIDES VAL, FORCING HIS ENEMY TO TURN IN THE SADDLE AND FIGHT AWKWARDLY···· SOONER OR LATER HE MUST GET OFF BALANCE.

IT HAPPENS, AND AS THE HUN GRASPS FOR HIS SADDLE, VAL CLOSES IN, HOOKS A TOE UNDER HIS ADVERSARY'S FOOT AND TUMBLES HIM OFF.

"I SHOULD KILL YOU," SAYS VAL, *"BUT I DON'T WANT TO SPOIL MY NEW CLOTHES·····TAKE THEM OFF!"*

132· 8-20-39

MEANWHILE, POOR SLITH IS HAVING TROUBLE - THE FALLEN TREE IS A BARRIER TO THE HORSES, BUT THE MEN HAVE DISMOUNTED AND COME SWARMING OVER IN PURSUIT

HEARING A NOISE VAL LOOKS UP AND THERE, COMING ROUND THE MOUNTAIN, IS SLITH FOLLOWED BY THE EVER-FAITHFUL SOCRATES AND FIFTY SHOUTING BARBARIANS!

HAL FOSTER

NEXT WEEK: "HOW THE RACE ENDED"

Prince Valiant

IN THE DAYS OF KING ARTHUR
BY
HAROLD R. FOSTER

CENTRAL ASIA — MONGOL — SAVE THIS STAMP

CENTRAL ASIA — TARTAR — SAVE THIS STAMP

Synopsis: VAL TOPPLES A GREAT PINE ACROSS THE TRAIL, SEPARATING A TROOP OF HUNS FROM THEIR CAPTAIN WHO HAPPENS TO WEAR A SUIT OF CLOTHES VAL WANTS. VAL GETS HIS OUTFIT, BUT ALL SLITH GETS IS SOME EXERCISE, AS FIFTY HUNS ON FOOT PURSUE HIM OVER THE MOUNTAIN.

AT VAL'S CALL SLITH COMES SPRINTING DOWN THE HILLSIDE.

"YOU ARE GOING THE WRONG WAY, VAL!"
"NO, I AM NOT. FOLLOW ME!"

THE HUNS LEAVE BEHIND TWO OF THEIR NUMBER TO CLEAR THE TRAIL — A TASK THEY NEVER COMPLETE······

···FOR VAL AND SLITH LEAP THE BARRIER, CUT THEM DOWN····

···AND STAMPEDE THEIR MOUNTS AND BAGGAGE ANIMALS UP THE PATH.

LEAVING THE TRAIL THEY CROSS THE VALLEY FLOOR AND DRIVE THEIR PLUNDER UP A SIDE CANYON.

AT THE NARROW PART THEY FELL TREES TO KEEP THE CAPTURED HORSES FROM ESCAPING.

CENTRAL ASIA — SYTHIAN — SAVE THIS STAMP

133: 8-27-39

AND THEN EXAMINE THEIR HAUL····WEALTH THERE IS IN PLENTY AND ARMS FOR A SMALL ARMY. VAL BECOMES THOUGHTFUL.

HAL FOSTER

"FOR NEARLY SIX YEARS THE HUN HAS ROBBED AND PILLAGED EUROPE·····
IT IS TIME NOW THAT SOME ONE ROBS THE HUN····I WONDER?"

NEXT WEEK: "THE LEGION OF HUN-HUNTERS"

CENTRAL ASIA — HUN — SAVE THIS STAMP

MOUNTAINEER · SAVE THIS STAMP

Prince Valiant
Registered U. S. Patent Office

IN THE DAYS OF KING ARTHUR
BY HAROLD R FOSTER

MOUNTAINEER · SAVE THIS STAMP

Synopsis: BY A GREAT STROKE OF LUCK AND DARING VAL AND SLITH STEAL THE HORSES AND PLUNDER OF A TROOP OF HUN RAIDERS. THERE ARE ARMS AND SUPPLIES FOR A REGIMENT AMONG THE LOOT. ALL VAL NEEDS IS THE REGIMENT TO FULFIL A DARING PLAN.

"SLITH, I NEED SOME FIGHTING MEN, REFUGEES OR BANDITS, SO LONG AS THEY HATE THE HUN. FIND THEM FOR ME."

HIGH UP IN THE HIDDEN VALLEYS THEY FIND SMALL FIELDS AND GARDENS, BUT NOWHERE A SIGN OF HABITATION.

"THEIR HOMES ARE HIDDEN FROM THE HUNS," SAYS SLITH, WHO TAKES A HORN FROM SOCRATES' PACK AND BLOWS A SHEPHERD'S CALL.

THEY ARE ANSWERED FROM A CAUTIOUS DISTANCE. "BRING ME TEN BRAVE FIGHTING MEN AND I WILL GIVE THEM ALL THE FOOD AND LOOT THEY CAN CARRY," CRIES VAL.

AN HOUR LATER SEVERAL STALWART MEN APPEAR. VAL SAYS:— "THE HUNS ROBBED YOU · · · I ROB THE HUNS. THE PLUNDER IS YOURS IF YOU CARE TO COME AND TAKE IT."

BACK TO THEIR HIDING-PLACE THEY GO AND EACH OF THE REFUGEES IS ALLOWED TO TAKE ALL HE CAN CARRY ON HIS BACK. SLITH YELPS IN PROTEST AT SUCH USELESS EXTRAVAGANCE.

"NO MAN IS EVER SATISFIED, SLITH. EVERY ONE WILL BE BACK AND MORE WILL COME AS THE NEWS IS SPREAD."

134: 9-3-39

AND RIGHT HE IS — SOON A CROWD OF WILD, HALF-STARVED MEN IS CLAMORING FOR FOOD. "I GO TO ROB THE HUN AGAIN TO-NIGHT, WHO WILL FOLLOW ME?"

Copr. 1939, King Features Syndicate, Inc., World rights reserved

OH! THE JOY THAT FILLS A WARRIOR'S HEART WHEN ONCE AGAIN HE LEADS FIGHTING MEN TO MEET A FOE!

NEXT WEEK—
THE HUN-HUNTERS

MOUNTAINEER · SAVE THIS STAMP

SIGNALS
THE HORN
SAVE THIS STAMP

Prince Valiant

IN THE DAYS OF
KING ARTHUR
BY
HAROLD R FOSTER

SIGNALS
SMOKE
SAVE THIS STAMP

Synopsis: FOR YEARS THE FEROCIOUS HUNS HAVE PILLAGED EUROPE UNHINDERED, BUT NOW THEY IN TURN ARE TO BE PILLAGED. FOR PRINCE VALIANT HAS RECRUITED A SMALL BAND OF REFUGEES AND BANDITS UNITED IN A COMMON HATRED OF THE HUN, AND HAS PLANNED A DARING RAID.

WHERE THE SIDE CANYON ENTERS THE WIDE VALLEY OF THE PASS VAL HALTS HIS LITTLE TROOP.

BELOW THEIR SENTINELS IS A WELL-WATERED MEADOW WHERE THOSE WHO CROSS THE PASS REST AT NIGHTFALL, WEARY FROM A HARD DAY'S TRAVEL.

DOWN FROM THE SNOWY HEIGHTS THAT EVENING COMES A CARAVAN LOADED WITH THE LOOT OF MONTHS OF RAIDING.

WEARILY THEY PITCH THEIR TENTS AND FLING THEMSELVES DOWN TO REST, UNAWARE THAT A GRIM-FACED TROOP IS QUIETLY APPROACHING.

SUDDENLY THERE IS A DRUMMING OF HOOFS - A WILD YELL AND VAL'S HUN-HUNTERS SPREAD PANIC AMONG THE BEWILDERED BARBARIANS.

ERE THE SCATTERED HUNS CAN ORGANIZE FOR DEFENSE THE BAGGAGE ANIMALS ARE LOADED - TENTS FIRED AND - THE CLATTERING HOOFS FADE AWAY INTO THE DARKNESS.

135: 9-10-39

DAWN FINDS THE RAIDERS, WILD WITH THE JOY OF SUCCESS, DRIVING THEIR RICH PLUNDER INTO THE SIDE VALLEY.

Copr 1939 King Features Syndicate, Inc. World rights reserved

BUT THE HAPPIEST OF ALL IS A CERTAIN YOUNG PRINCE, AS HE ACKNOWLEDGES THE CHEERS OF HIS VICTORIOUS MEN.

NEXT WEEK
THE HUN-HUNTERS CONTINUED

SIGNALS
THE BRAZIER
SAVE THIS STAMP

CESARIO
THE HORSEMAN
VAL'S LIEUTENANTS

Prince Valiant

IN THE DAYS OF KING ARTHUR
BY
HAROLD R FOSTER

Registered U. S. Patent Office.

DE GATIN
THE ARCHER
SAVE THIS STAMP

Synopsis: ONCE AGAIN THE HIDDEN VALLEY IS FILLED WITH RICH PLUNDER AND VAL'S TIRED HUN HUNTERS SLEEP AND DREAM OF MORE AND GREATER RAIDS WHILE THEIR DEFEATED FOES FLEE DOWN THE PASS IN THE DARKNESS TO SPREAD A WARNING.

FOR YEARS THESE MEN HAVE BEEN HUNTED REFUGEES FROM HUNNISH BRUTALITY; NOW THEY ARE CONQUERORS, WELL-FED AND SLEEPING IN TENTS. THE TIDE AT LAST IS CHANGING.

IN THE MORNING VAL DISMISSES HIS MEN – EACH TO TAKE AS MUCH OF THE PLUNDER AS HE CAN CARRY. HE IS NO FOOL, HE KNOWS THE NEWS OF HIS SUCCESS AND GENEROSITY WILL SPREAD LIKE WILD-FIRE THROUGH THE HILLS

THE RESPONSE IS ENTHUSIASTIC – THE MEN OF THE HILLS HAVE AT LAST FOUND A LEADER WHO PROMISES THEM FOOD, FIGHTING AND REVENGE⋯A FINE TROOP GATHERS.

FIRST VAL SENDS OUT SPIES TO GATHER NEWS AND LEARNS THAT SMALL BANDS OF HUNS ARE NO LONGER USING THE PASS, BUT ARE GATHERING IN LARGE NUMBERS BEFORE CROSSING.

WITH SOCRATES CARRYING A WEEK'S PROVISIONS VAL AND SLITH MAKE A CAREFUL STUDY OF THE PASS AND THE SURROUNDING COUNTRY⋯⋯

⋯⋯AND FIND AN EASILY DEFENDED CANYON JUST OFF THE PASS. HERE THEY CONSTRUCT A BARRICADE.

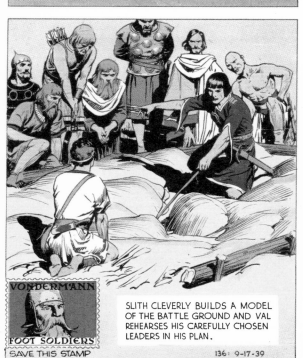

136: 9-17-39

SLITH CLEVERLY BUILDS A MODEL OF THE BATTLE GROUND AND VAL REHEARSES HIS CAREFULLY CHOSEN LEADERS IN HIS PLAN.

HAL FOSTER

Copr. 1939, King Features Syndicate, Inc., World rights reserved.

AT LAST COMES WORD THAT THE HUNS ARE ON THE MARCH, A THOUSAND FIGHTING MEN LEADING, THEN THE BAGGAGE TRAIN FOLLOWED BY FIVE HUNDRED MORE WARRIORS. THE DAY HAS AT LAST ARRIVED. VAL CALLS HIS THREE HUNDRED INTO ACTION!

NEXT WEEK:
"AT THE BARRICADE"

Prince Valiant

IN THE DAYS OF KING ARTHUR
BY
HAROLD R FOSTER

HUNTING
THE FALCON
SAVE THIS STAMP

HUNTING
DEER HOUND
SAVE THIS STAMP

Synopsis: PRINCE VALIANT'S BAND OF 'HUN HUNTERS' HAVE MADE THE PASS SO DANGEROUS THAT THE HUNS NO LONGER DARE CROSS IT UNTIL THEY HAVE GATHERED A CONSIDERABLE FORCE TO GUARD THEIR RICH PLUNDER.

HIDDEN IN THEIR NARROW GORGE VAL'S HARDY TROOP AWAIT THE SIGNAL THAT WILL WARN THEM OF THE HUN'S APPROACH.

UP THE WINDING VALLEY COMES THE HUN CARAVAN-GUARDED BY A THOUSAND WARRIORS IN FRONT AND FIVE HUNDRED IN THE REAR.

JUST AS THE BAGGAGE TRAIN REACHES THE MOUTH OF VAL'S GORGE A DISTANT HORN SOUNDS AND ACROSS THE WIDE VALLEY SWEEPS A TROOP OF HORSEMEN.....

.....STRAIGHT FOR THE HUNS THEY GALLOP, THEN, SEEING THE STRENGTH OF THEIR VICTIMS, TURN AND FLEE. WITH A WILD SHOUT THE VANGUARD SETS OFF IN PURSUIT.

WITH THE VANGUARD DECOYED FAR OUT ACROSS THE VALLEY AND THE REARGUARD STRUNG OUT BEHIND ON A NARROW TRAIL VAL AND HIS MEN SUDDENLY APPEAR AND TAKE CHARGE OF THE BAGGAGE TRAIN.......

......DRIVING IT OFF THE TRAIL UP THE GORGE AND PAST THEIR BARRICADE, WHICH IS AT ONCE CLOSED.

MEANWHILE THE PATH IN FRONT OF THE REARGUARD IS BLOCKED WITH DEBRIS—

137: 9-24-39

FAR ACROSS THE VALLEY THE HUN VANGUARD DISCOVERS THEY ARE CHASING ONLY MOUNTED BOYS AND OLD MEN—AND—TOO LATE, REALIZE THEY HAVE BEEN TRICKED.

HAL FOSTER

WILD WITH RAGE AT THE HOAX PUT UPON THEM THEY GALLOP BACK ONLY TO FIND THEIR PLUNDER DRIVEN UP THE GORGE AND THE WAY BLOCKED BY A BARRICADE!
NEXT WEEK "THE VANISHED CARAVAN"

SHIELDS
WOOD — IRON
SAVE THIS STAMP

SHIELDS
BRONZE
SAVE THIS STAMP

Synopsis: PRINCE VALIANT'S PLAN WORKS PERFECTLY; THE HUNS ARE TRICKED INTO LEAVING THEIR BAGGAGE TRAIN UNGUARDED AND THE BAND OF "HUN-HUNTERS" SWOOP DOWN AND DRIVE IT UP THEIR FORTIFIED GORGE.

UNABLE TO STORM THE BARRICADE THE HUN CHIEFTAIN ORDERS HIS MEN TO DISMOUNT AND CLIMB AROUND IT.

BUT VAL IS READY – SOON THE BARRICADE IS A RAGING MASS OF FLAME, AND HIS MEN RETREATING.

THOUGH A DEMON WARRIOR ON HORSEBACK, THE HUN IS A POOR FIGHTER ON FOOT AND IT WILL BE HOURS BEFORE THEY CAN GET THEIR HORSES PAST THE BURNING BARRIER.

MEANWHILE, THE CARAVAN HAS BEEN DIVIDED AND SENT OUT OF THE VALLEY BY A DOZEN DIFFERENT PATHS.

WHEN AT LAST THE HUNS RIDE UP THE VALLEY IT IS EMPTY! ONLY A STINGING FLIGHT OF ARROWS COMES INCESSANTLY FROM AN INVISIBLE FOE.

RIGHT UP TO THE HEAD OF THE VALLEY GO THE HUNS WITH NEVER A SIGN OF THEIR FABULOUSLY RICH CARAVAN. IN RAGE AND DESPAIR THEY RETURN.

SHIELDS
LEATHER – BRONZE
SAVE THIS STAMP

138 10-1-39

AND THEIR RETREAT GIVES VAL ANOTHER SURPRISING VICTORY, BUT HE REMAINS CALM – THE HUN WILL SEEK REVENGE!

FOR THREE DAYS VAL KEEPS HIS MEN IN HAND UNTIL THE LAST OF THE NOW STARVING HUNS HAS CROSSED THE PASS....THEN THEY HOLD A VICTORY FEAST.

Copr. 1939, King Features Syndicate, Inc., World rights reserved

IN FAR OFF PANNONIA THE NEWS OF VAL'S RAIDS CAUSES GREAT ANGER. *"THE HUN MUST BE FEARED AND RESPECTED!"* CRIES THE GREAT KHAN AND CALLS UP AN ARMY.

NEXT WEEK: **TROUBLE!**

SHIELDS
RAW HIDE
SAVE THIS STAMP

TRISTRAM
SAVE THIS STAMP

KALLA KHAN
SAVE THIS STAMP

Synopsis: UNDER PRINCE VALIANT'S DARING LEADERSHIP THE "LEGION OF HUN-HUNTERS" HAS STRUCK AGAIN AND AGAIN AS THE HUNS CROSS THE PASS; RUNNING OFF THEIR HORSES, THEIR PLUNDER AND THEIR SUPPLIES, WITH NEVER A CHANCE TO STRIKE BACK AT THEIR NIMBLE FOE, THE HUNS ARE LEFT TO STARVE IN A WILDERNESS OF THEIR OWN MAKING.

THE RAGE OF KALLA KHAN IS TERRIBLE AS THE FAMISHED SURVIVORS STRAGGLE BACK INTO PANNONIA WITH TIDINGS OF STILL MORE DEFEATS.

THE KHAN SUMMONS "KARNAK, THE FEROCIOUS," AND SAYS; "TAKE AN ARMY, CLEAR THE PASS AND FORTIFY IT. TWO MOONS FROM TO-DAY RETURN WITH THE HEAD OF PRINCE VALIANT!"

"YONDER ARE TWO STAKES.... ON ONE IS THE HEAD OF A DEFEATED GENERAL. THE OTHER IS FOR THE HEAD OF PRINCE VALIANT..... OR YOUR OWN!"

ON THE PLAIN BELOW THE PASS THE VAST HUN ARMY STARTS BUILDING A FORTIFIED CAMP.

BUT NEWS OF VAL'S ASTOUNDING SUCCESS HAS SPREAD FAR AND WIDE AND HIS ARMY GROWS. EVEN SLY VALENTINIAN SENDS 500 ARMED AND MOUNTED KNIGHTS FROM ROME......

......AND FROM SPAIN THE KING SENDS A THOUSAND HARD-FIGHTING VISIGOTHS WITH ARMS AND MONEY.

KARNAK
SAVE THIS STAMP

BUT, BEST OF ALL, FROM KING ARTHUR'S COURT IN FAR-OFF BRITAIN, COME TWO BATTERED KNIGHTS ERRANT.... MIGHTY TRISTRAM AND MERRY SIR GAWAIN!

139-10-8-39

TRISTRAM SEEKING IN HARDSHIP AND ADVENTURE TO FORGET FAIR ISOLDE AND GAWAIN TO ESCAPE KING ARTHUR'S DISPLEASURE AT HIS MISCHIEF.

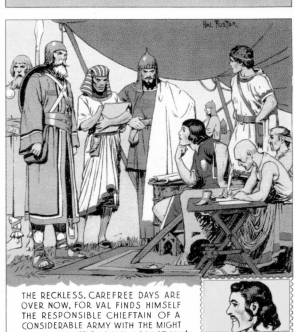

THE RECKLESS, CAREFREE DAYS ARE OVER NOW, FOR VAL FINDS HIMSELF THE RESPONSIBLE CHIEFTAIN OF A CONSIDERABLE ARMY WITH THE MIGHT OF THE HUN NATION PITTED AGAINST HIM!

NEXT WEEK— **TREACHERY!**

SIR GAWAIN
SAVE THIS STAMP

Prince Valiant

IN THE DAYS OF KING ARTHUR
BY HAROLD R FOSTER

Synopsis: THE RAPIDLY GROWING FORCES UNDER PRINCE VALIANT'S LEADERSHIP HOLD THE PASS, BUT IN THE PLAIN BELOW THE HUNS' VAST ARMY HAS BUILT A STRONGLY FORTIFIED BASE AND MORE MEN AND SUPPLIES ARRIVE DAILY.

HUN SCOUTS TRY DESPERATELY TO FIND OUT THE STRENGTH OF THE "HUN-HUNTERS."

IN THE EXCITEMENT OF THESE SKIRMISHES VAL FORGETS HIS CARES, AND ONCE AGAIN GOES CRASHING INTO THE FRAY, SIDE BY SIDE WITH TRISTRAM AND GAWAIN!

BUT SPIES ARE BEING FOUND IN GREAT NUMBERS, COMING UP BEHIND THEM FROM THE FAR SIDE OF THE PASS — FROM A CAPTURED OFFICER VAL LEARNS THE CAUSE.....

...TWO DAYS' RIDE TO THE SOUTH IS A PASS GUARDED BY THE BEAUTIFUL WALLED CITY OF PANDARIS. DUKE CESARIO HELD THE PASS AGAINST THE HUN, BUT HIS COUSIN, DISCARO, AIDED BY TREACHERY AND THE HUNS, IMPRISONS CESARIO, SETS HIMSELF UP AS TYRANT AND OPENS THE PASS TO THE BARBARIANS.

LOOKING DOWN UPON THEIR ENEMY'S PREPARATIONS, THEY ESTIMATE THAT IT WILL BE TWO MOONS BEFORE THEY ARE READY TO ATTACK. WITH THE ODDS ALREADY 20 TO 1 AGAINST THEM, THE "HUN-HUNTERS'" POSITION WILL BE HOPELESS IF THEY ARE ATTACKED FROM THE REAR ALSO.

HAL FOSTER

140. 10-15-39

DESPITE THE OBJECTIONS OF HIS COUNCIL, VAL SETS OUT FOR PANDARIS WITH A FORCE CONSISTING ONLY OF NIMBLE SLITH AND LONG-EARED SOCRATES!

NEXT WEEK—
PANDARIS!

Synopsis: THE BEAUTIFUL WHITE-WALLED CITY OF PANDARIS STOOD GUARD OVER THE SOUTHERN PASS SO LONG AS BRAVE DUKE CESARIO REIGNED. BUT THE TREACHERY OF HIS COUSIN, PISCARO, OVERTHEW CESARIO AND NOW THE HUNS SWARM THROUGH TO ATTACK THE "HUN-HUNTERS" FROM BEHIND. VAL AND SLITH SET OUT FOR PANDARIS.

A BITING WIND IS MOANING THROUGH THE HIGH PASS AND THEY CROSS IN SAFETY, OBSCURED BY THE SWIRLING SNOW.

IN THE FRIENDLY DARKNESS THEY DRIFT SILENTLY PAST THE SMALL HUN ENCAMPMENTS ON THE FAR SIDE OF THE PASS.

SEVERAL MILES FROM PANDARIS VAL HALTS AT THE HOME OF ONE GUIDO, A FAITHFUL FRIEND OF CESARIO, FOR REST AND INFORMATION.

"PISCARO IS A CRUEL TYRANT, WEAK AND VICIOUS. THE PEOPLE OF PANDARIS WOULD RESTORE BRAVE CESARIO TO POWER, BUT THEIR CITY IS FILLED WITH HUNS AND HE WHO RAISES HIS VOICE AGAINST PISCARO IS SWIFTLY MURDERED."

DRESSED AS PEDDLERS, VAL, SLITH AND SOCRATES APPROACH THE FAIR CITY, ITS SPIRES AND DOMES GLEAMING IN THE SUNLIGHT.

"WHAT IS YOUR BUSINESS WITHIN OUR CITY?" DEMANDS THE OFFICER AT THE GATE. "WE ARE MERCHANTS COME TO CHEAT THE HUNS," ANSWERS VAL BOLDLY. LOOKING CAUTIOUSLY AROUND, THE OFFICER WHISPERS. "PASS, FRIEND!"

WITHIN THE CITY IS THE BROODING SILENCE OF AN UNHAPPY PEOPLE. THE TWO FRIENDS ARE MOVING TOWARD THE PALACE, WHEN TRUMPETS SOUND.....

AND THE BRUTAL SOLDIERS CLEAR A PATH AMONG THE PEOPLE, AS THE DUKE RIDES FORTH!

NEXT WEEK—
VAL'S DEFIANCE!

Synopsis: PRINCE VALIANT AND SLITH TRAVEL TO PANDARIS TO FIND OUT WHY THAT WALLED CITY SHOULD LET THE HUNS PASS TO ATTACK HIS "HUN-HUNTERS" IN THE REAR. HE FINDS THAT TREACHEROUS PISCARO HAS SEIZED THE DUKE CESARIO AND ASSUMED COMMAND OF THE CITY.

"KNEEL IN THE DUST, SONS OF DOGS. HIS HIGHNESS APPROACHES!" CRY THE SOLDIERS, AS THEY CLEAR A PATH WITH THEIR RODS.

THE FALSE DUKE RIDES BY, DAINTILY WAVING A PERFUMED TASSEL BEFORE HIS WEAK, VINDICTIVE FACE.

"KNEEL, SIR," WHISPER THE CITIZENS. "IT IS DEATH MOST TERRIBLE TO OFFEND THE DUKE." BUT VAL IS A PRINCE AND KNIGHT OF THE ROUND TABLE AND WILL KNEEL TO NO SUCH TYRANT! "I'VE SEEN BETTER MEN IN MY FATHER'S STABLES!" QUOTH HE.

THE SOMBER EYE OF THE TYRANT FALLS ON THE ERECT FIGURE OF THE PRINCE AND HIS FACE FLUSHES WITH RAGE. "BREAK HIS LEGS THAT HE MAY BE GLAD TO KNEEL," HE COMMANDS.

"THANKS FOR REMINDING ME OF MY LEGS," SHOUTS VAL AND PROMPTLY USES THEM.

HE IS RAPIDLY OUTRUNNING HIS PURSUERS WHEN, BY ILL LUCK, HE DODGES INTO A BLIND STREET FROM WHICH THERE IS NO OUTLET.

THE NOISE OF PURSUIT IS DRAWING DESPERATELY NEAR WHEN SUDDENLY HE IS SEIZED BY A STRONG HAND AND JERKED INTO A DOORWAY.

142 10-29-39   Copr. 1939 King Features Syndicate, Inc., World rights reserved

VAL WHIPS OUT HIS READY DAGGER, BUT A CALM VOICE SAYS: "WILL YOU TRUST YOURSELF TO ME OR TO THE SOLDIERS OUTSIDE?"

NEXT WEEK—
THE "LIBERATORS"

Prince Valiant

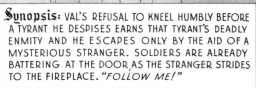

Synopsis: VAL'S REFUSAL TO KNEEL HUMBLY BEFORE A TYRANT HE DESPISES EARNS THAT TYRANT'S DEADLY ENMITY AND HE ESCAPES ONLY BY THE AID OF A MYSTERIOUS STRANGER. SOLDIERS ARE ALREADY BATTERING AT THE DOOR, AS THE STRANGER STRIDES TO THE FIREPLACE. *"FOLLOW ME!"*

HE DISAPPEARS UPWARD IN THE DARKNESS AND VAL QUICKLY FOLLOWS—HIS GROPING HANDS FIND THE NICHES AND HE MOUNTS RAPIDLY.

THEY EMERGE INTO THE ADJOINING HOUSE. *"THIS IS THE SECRET MEETING-PLACE OF THE 'LIBERATORS.' I TRUST YOUR HATRED OF PISCARO WILL MAKE YOU ONE OF US."*

THE "LIBERATORS" ARE FAITHFUL FRIENDS OF DUKE CESARIO, FORCED BY PISCARO'S WEAK FEROCITY TO SEEK SAFETY IN DISGUISE AND HIDING.... AND IN THEIR HIDING-PLACES THEY PLOT.

VAL LEARNS THAT THE CITIZENS LOATHE THE CRUEL PISCARO, BUT THE MENACING SHADOW OF THE HUN KEEPS THEM COWED. ONLY THROUGH THE DEATH OF PISCARO AND LIBERATION OF DUKE CESARIO CAN VAL EXPECT HELP FOR HIS TROOPS.

ALL THROUGH THE DAY AND INTO THE NIGHT THE SOLDIERS SEARCH FOR PRINCE VALIANT, FOR THEY FEAR THEIR MASTER'S WRATH IF THEY FAIL.

LIKE A GHOST SLITH HAUNTS THE STREETS AND ALLEYS, SEARCHING DAY AND NIGHT FOR HIS FRIEND.

FOR A BRIEF WHILE VAL REMAINS IN HIDING THEN, DONNING THE GARB OF A HUN WARRIOR, HE VENTURES FORTH.

BUT, NO MATTER WHAT CLOTHES HE WEARS, THERE IS ONE THING HE CANNOT DISGUISE; HE IS A KING'S SON AND LOOKS IT EVERY INCH!

143 11-5-39

HE IS RECOGNIZED IMMEDIATELY, OVERPOWERED AND DRAGGED OFF TO THE PALACE... AND PISCARO'S VENGEANCE!

NEXT WEEK—
PISCARO'S TORTURE ROOM!

A TORMENTOR
SAVE THIS STAMP

Prince Valiant

IN THE DAYS OF KING ARTHUR
BY
HAROLD R FOSTER

A TORTURER
SAVE THIS STAMP

Synopsis: THE EVIL PISCARO HAS TAKEN THE CITY PANDARIS FROM DUKE CESARIO THROUGH TREACHERY AND THE HUNS' AID. CESARIO IS THROWN INTO PRISON AND THE HUNS ARE FREE TO ATTACK VAL'S TROOPS FROM THE REAR. VAL HAS EARNED THE ENMITY OF PISCARO.

A DISGUISE CANNOT HIDE HIS PRINCELY BEARING; VAL IS RECOGNIZED AND QUICKLY CAPTURED.

IN A ROOM DRUGGED WITH THE VAPOR OF PERFUME AND INCENSE VAL STANDS BEFORE PISCARO AND MEETS THE UNBLINKING HATRED IN HIS EYES.

"SO - THEY HAVE BROUGHT YOU TO ME AT LAST! EVERYONE FEARS ME....ONLY YOU DEFY ME....BUT YOU HAVE NOT YET VISITED MY TORTURE CHAMBER. SOON YOU WILL WHIMPER FOR THE RELIEF OF DEATH," AND PISCARO SNICKERS.

VAL IS DRAGGED BRUTALLY DOWN TO A DUNGEON CELL.......

.......AND CHAINED TO THE DAMP, COLD WALL.

DEATH AND HORROR LURK IN THE VERY AIR OF THIS GRUESOME PLACE. VAL'S MIND IS BUSY WITH PLANS FOR ESCAPE WHEN HE IS STARTLED BY A VOICE.

THROUGH A SMALL WINDOW BETWEEN THE CELLS PEERS A PALE FACE. "I AM DUKE CESARIO," HE WHISPERS. "THE SCREAMS OF PISCARO'S VICTIMS ARE DRIVING ME MAD. IS THERE ANY HOPE OF RESCUE?"

VAL TELLS HIM OF THE "LIBERATORS" WHILE A SPY LISTENS OUTSIDE. FOR THESE WINDOWS BETWEEN THE CELLS ARE FOR THE PURPOSE OF ENCOURAGING TALK.

AT FIRST VAL'S NIMBLE MIND IS BUSY WITH SCHEMES FOR ESCAPE, BUT AS THE DAYS DRAG INTO WEEKS HE BECOMES NUMBED WITH MISERY. PISCARO'S VOICE AWAKENS HIM: "YOUR TIME HAS COME!"

NEXT WEEK-
THE RACK!

144 11-12-39

Prince Valiant

IN THE DAYS OF
KING ARTHUR
BY
HAROLD R FOSTER

Synopsis: TO PREVENT HIS "LEGION OF HUN-HUNTERS" FROM BEING SURROUNDED VAL FINDS IT NECESSARY TO RESCUE THE DUKE CESARIO FROM THE HANDS OF TREACHEROUS PISCARO. UNFORTUNATELY, PRINCE VALIANT, HIMSELF, FALLS INTO PISCARO'S POWER AND HAS SPENT TWO WEEKS CRUELLY CHAINED IN A FILTHY CELL.

"AND NOW THE TIME HAS COME FOR MY SWEET REVENGE," SAYS PISCARO RUBBING HIS COLD HANDS SOFTLY TOGETHER.

THE TORMENTORS STRETCH VAL'S STRONG YOUNG BODY UPON THE RACK AND DRAW THE CHAINS TIGHT, WHILE PISCARO SNICKERS.

"NOW TELL ME WHO THE LIBERATORS ARE....TELL ME WHO PLOTS AGAINST ME, BEFORE YOUR BONES CRACK. NAME THOSE WHO WOULD FREE CESARIO, OR SLOWLY WILL I TEAR YOUR BEAUTIFUL BODY ASUNDER."

THE MERCILESS TORMENTORS BEAR DOWN ON THEIR LEVERS. THERE COMES A HORRIBLE SNAP. VAL SCREAMS, "I'LL TELL, OH! I'LL TELL!"..... HE MOANS AND FAINTS.

"CLUMSY FOOLS!" SHRIEKS PISCARO, "IF YOU HAVE KILLED HIM IT IS THE RACK FOR BOTH OF YOU! REVIVE HIM AND WHEN HE CAN TALK, CALL ME."

LATER, WHEN THEY CALL HIM, HE SAYS, "AFTER I HAVE HIS CONFESSION YOU MAY BEAT HIM TO DEATH."

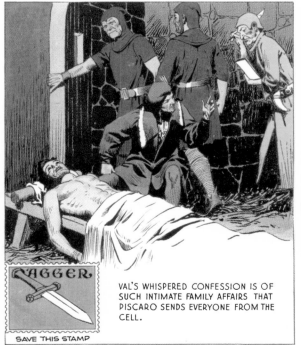

VAL'S WHISPERED CONFESSION IS OF SUCH INTIMATE FAMILY AFFAIRS THAT PISCARO SENDS EVERYONE FROM THE CELL.

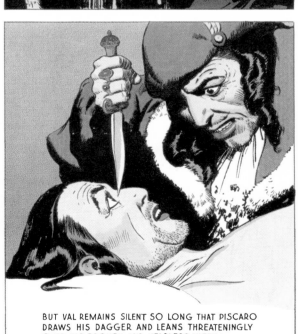

BUT VAL REMAINS SILENT SO LONG THAT PISCARO DRAWS HIS DAGGER AND LEANS THREATENINGLY OVER HIS BROKEN AND HELPLESS VICTIM.

145 11-19-39

HELPLESS? WELL, NOT QUITE...FOR TWO STRONG HANDS SEIZE HIM IN A VICE-LIKE GRIP AND HE IS BORNE SILENTLY TO THE FLOOR.

NEXT WEEK—
A NEW PISCARO.

HAL FOSTER

Synopsis: PRINCE VALIANT'S ARMY NEEDS THE HELP OF CESARIO, DUKE OF PANDARIS, BUT BOTH VAL AND THE DUKE HAVE FALLEN INTO THE POWER OF PISCARO AND, TO GET A CONFESSION, VAL HAS BEEN BROKEN UPON THE RACK.

BUT HIS BROKEN, HELPLESS VICTIM COMES SUDDENLY TO LIFE AND PISCARO IS SEIZED IN A TERRIBLE GRIP.

THE HATRED BORN OF WEEKS OF MISERY GOES INTO THAT ONE SMASHING BLOW

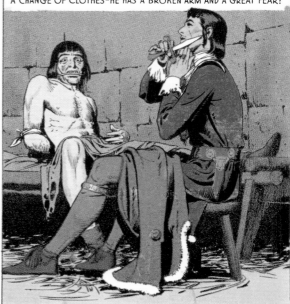

WHEN, FINALLY, PISCARO RETURNS TO CONSCIOUSNESS A GREAT CHANGE HAS TAKEN PLACE—HE HAS HAD A HAIR-CUT, A SHAVE AND A CHANGE OF CLOTHES—HE HAS A BROKEN ARM AND A GREAT FEAR!

"THOUGHT YOU HAD BROKEN ME, DID YOU? TAUNTS VAL. "MY BONES DIDN'T BREAK – I JUST CLICKED MY TEETH AND SNAPPED MY FINGERS....THE REST WAS ACTING!"

REMOVING THE GAG VAL HITS HIM AGAIN ON THE CHIN TO KEEP HIM QUIET. THEN, IMITATING PISCARO'S MINCING WALK, LEAVES THE DUNGEON.

THROUGH HIS LITTLE WINDOW DUKE CESARIO SEES THE WHOLE ASTONISHING SCENE......EVEN NOW HE CAN HARDLY BELIEVE THAT THE MOANING FIGURE ON THE COT IS NOT VAL....AND HOPE COMES AGAIN TO THE DUKE.

WITH HEAD DOWN VAL QUICKLY MINCES ACROSS THE BRILLIANT HALL AND TO PISCARO'S ROOMS.

"BRING CESARIO HERE AND CHAIN HIM TO THE WALL!"

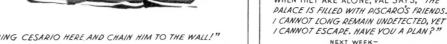

HAL FOSTER

WHEN THEY ARE ALONE, VAL SAYS, "THE PALACE IS FILLED WITH PISCARO'S FRIENDS. I CANNOT LONG REMAIN UNDETECTED, YET I CANNOT ESCAPE. HAVE YOU A PLAN?"

NEXT WEEK—
THE PLAN.

Synopsis: VAL TRICKS PISCARO INTO THINKING HIM HELPLESS AND PISCARO ENTERS THE CELL ALONE. VAL LEAVES, DRESSED IN PISCARO'S GARMENTS, WHILE THE PETTY TYRANT STAYS TO FACE THE DOOM HE HAS ORDERED FOR VAL. STILL POSING AS PISCARO, VAL ORDERS THE REAL DUKE BROUGHT FROM THE DUNGEON AND CHAINED TO THE WALL

"THE CASTLE IS FILLED WITH PISCARO'S FRIENDS. NOT ONLY MUST WE ESCAPE, BUT YOU MUST ONCE MORE RULE IN THE CITY OF PANDARIS."

"I HAVE IT!.... WE CANNOT GO TO YOUR FRIENDS, BUT WE CAN BRING YOUR FRIENDS TO US!"

"GET BACK IN YOUR CHAINS, CESARIO, WHILE I SUMMON THE GUARDS, AND REMEMBER...I AM PISCARO AND I HAVE FORCED YOU TO BETRAY YOUR FOLLOWERS."

"MY DEAR COUSIN HAS AT LAST DECIDED TO BETRAY HIS FAITHFUL FRIENDS...TAKE DOWN THEIR NAMES AND ARREST THEM. BY TO-MORROW MY RULE WILL BE UNQUESTIONED!"

"BUT REMEMBER - ARREST EACH ONE SECRETLY AND LOCK THEM UP UNHARMED, IN THE ARMORY."

AT THE STROKE OF MIDNIGHT THE ORDER IS QUIETLY CARRIED OUT.

INTO THE GLOOMY, ECHOING ARMORY ARE HERDED ALL WHO HAD REMAINED FAITHFUL TO DUKE CESARIO.

CREST OF PISCARO — SAVE THIS STAMP

NEXT WEEK
A MESSENGER COMES

HELMET OF CESARIO — SAVE THIS STAMP

Prince Valiant

PISCARO
SAVE THIS STAMP

IN THE DAYS OF KING ARTHUR
BY
HAROLD R FOSTER

VAL'S DISGUISE
SAVE THIS STAMP

Synopsis: STILL POSING AS PISCARO, VAL RESCUES THE REAL DUKE CESARIO FROM THE DUNGEON. EACH MOMENT THEY EXPECT DISCOVERY.... VAL ORDERS THE ARREST OF ALL WHO HAVE DARED REMAIN FAITHFUL TO CESARIO AND THEY ARE IMPRISONED IN THE GREAT ARMORY.

"AH! SIR VALIANT, I SEE YOUR PLAN NOW—IN NO OTHER WAY COULD MY FRIENDS ENTER THIS STRONGHOLD."

THEIR PLANNING IS INTERRUPTED BY THE MASTER OF THE DUNGEONS ..."WE HAVE FINISHED WITH PRINCE VALIANT AS YOU DIRECTED, YOUR EXCELLENCY, HE DIED SCREAMING VERY SATISFACTORILY."

"FOOL! I AM PRINCE VALIANT. THAT WAS PISCARO YOU KILLED!"

IN THOSE TWO BLAZING EYES THE MASTER TORTURER READS CLEARLY HIS DOOM—HE LEAPS FOR THE DOOR JUST A SECOND TOO LATE.

"IT IS AN UNPLEASANT FACT THAT YOU AND I SO RESEMBLE THE WORLD'S TWO MEANEST SCOUNDRELS THAT WE CAN ACT THEIR PARTS."

IN AN AGONY OF DESPAIR SLITH WAITS DAY AFTER DAY FOR SOME WORD OF HIS MASTER'S FATE.

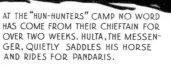

QUESTIONER
SAVE THIS STAMP

AT THE "HUN-HUNTERS" CAMP NO WORD HAS COME FROM THEIR CHIEFTAIN FOR OVER TWO WEEKS. HULTA, THE MESSENGER, QUIETLY SADDLES HIS HORSE AND RIDES FOR PANDARIS.

HE SOON FINDS THE HAGGARD, SLEEPLESS SLITH AND LEARNS FROM HIM OF VAL'S CAPTURE BY PISCARO.

148 12-10-39

WITH THE SEEMING RECKLESSNESS OF THE BORN HORSEMAN HULTA SPEEDS BACK TO THE CAMP.

HAL FOSTER

NEXT WEEK—
IN THE ARMORY

CESARIO'S DISGUISE
SAVE THIS STAMP

HOOKED SPEAR PULLS SHIELD DOWN
SAVE THIS STAMP

Prince Valiant

IN THE DAYS OF KING ARTHUR
BY Harold R Foster

SHIELD DAGGER
SAVE THIS STAMP

Synopsis: OVER STEEP MOUNTAIN PATHS RIDES HULTA, BACK TO THE CAMP WHERE THE "HUN-HUNTERS" AWAIT THE ATTACK OF THE HUN ARMY UNDER "KARNAK, THE FEROCIOUS." TO THE CAPTAINS HE REPORTS—

"PRINCE VALIANT, OUR FEARLESS LEADER, IS HELD PRISONER BY FALSE DUKE PISCARO, HIS FATE UNKNOWN.... IF WE TURN FROM THE HUN ARMY TO ATTACK PISCARO'S WALLED CITY OF PANDARIS WE WILL BE CAUGHT BETWEEN TWO ENEMIES."

ALL AGREE THAT HULTA SPEAKS TRUE..... BUT LATER THEY SPEAK AS FOLLOWS-- SAYS SIR GAWAIN:- "I BELIEVE I SHALL RIDE TO PANDARIS AND HAVE THIS SWORD SHARPENED," AND TRISTRAM REMARKS:- SPLENDID WEATHER FOR RIDING, I'LL JOIN YOU!"

TO HIS SECOND IN COMMAND VONDERMAN OF THE FOOT-SOLDIERS SAYS:- "TAKE CHARGE WHILE I LEARN MORE ABOUT HORSEBACK-RIDING!"

CESARIO, THE HORSEMAN REMARKS; "MY WAR-HORSE GROWS STIFF FROM LACK OF EXERCISE, I MUST ATTEND TO IT AT ONCE!"

DE GATIN OF THE ARCHERS SHOUTS; "I GROW WEARY OF THIS WAITING FOR THE HUN ATTACK, I AM OFF FOR A FEW DAYS OF HUNTING!"

BUT YOUNG HULTA, THE MESSENGER, SAYS NOTHING AS USUAL... HE HAS ALREADY LEFT TO JOIN HIS FRIEND, SLITH, IN PANDARIS!

SO IT IS NOT STRANGE THAT THEY ALL MEET ON THE ROAD TO PANDARIS A FEW HOURS LATER!

MEANWHILE, WITHIN THE PALACE, VAL, DISGUISED AS PISCARO AND DUKE CESARIO IN THE GARMENT OF THE LATE CHIEF TORTURER, PREPARE TO PUT THEIR PLAN TO THE TEST.

ORDERING THE ENTIRE PALACE GUARD AS ESCORT, THEY PASS UNDETECTED THROUGH THE CROWDED PALACE INTO THE COURTYARD.

"ARE YOU SURE THE PRISONERS ARE SECURELY CHAINED? HAVE THEY BEEN SEARCHED FOR WEAPONS? THEN GIVE ME THE KEYS THAT I MAY BE SURE."

"MY CHIEF TORTURER WILL HELP ME AMUSE MYSELF WITH MY MANY PRISONERS - WAIT OUTSIDE, READY TO ANSWER MY SLIGHTEST CALL."

149 12-17-39   Copr. 1939, King Features Syndicate, Inc., World rights reserved.

"SPLENDID," GRINS VAL, "ARMS AND ARMOR AND FIFTY OF YOUR GOOD FRIENDS TO USE THEM...TO WORK!"

Hal Foster

NEXT WEEK — HOUSECLEANING.

THE MACE
SAVE THIS STAMP

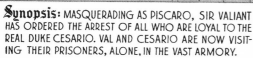

Synopsis: MASQUERADING AS PISCARO, SIR VALIANT HAS ORDERED THE ARREST OF ALL WHO ARE LOYAL TO THE REAL DUKE CESARIO. VAL AND CESARIO ARE NOW VISITING THEIR PRISONERS, ALONE, IN THE VAST ARMORY.

"CAUTION YOUR FRIENDS TO ABSOLUTE SILENCE AND THEN REVEAL YOURSELF TO THEM, CESARIO."

WHISPERED GREETINGS WITH THEIR NOBLE LEADER OF OLD, THEN HURRIEDLY EACH ONE ARMS HIMSELF..........

"OFFICER, MARCH THE GUARD IN AND FORM AGAINST THE SOUTH WALL."

WITHIN THE DIM BUILDING THEY FIND NOT HELPLESS PRISONERS, BUT FIFTY ARMED KNIGHTS AND THE GRIM-FACED DUKE. "I WILL JUDGE OF YOUR LOYALTY LATER, UNTIL THEN YOU WILL BE LOCKED IN THIS ARMORY."

THE FRIENDS AND FOLLOWERS OF SLY PISCARO ARE STARTLED TO SEE HIM LEAD A TROOP OF FULLY ARMED KNIGHTS ACROSS THE GREAT HALL TO THE DUCAL THRONE.

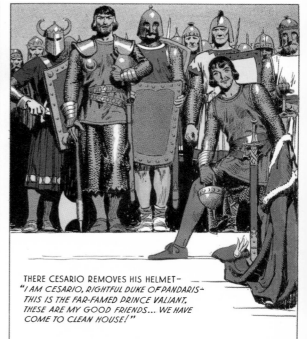

THERE CESARIO REMOVES HIS HELMET— "I AM CESARIO, RIGHTFUL DUKE OF PANDARIS— THIS IS THE FAR-FAMED PRINCE VALIANT. THESE ARE MY GOOD FRIENDS... WE HAVE COME TO CLEAN HOUSE!"

DOWN THE DUSTY ROAD INTO PANDARIS COMES TRISTRAM, GAWAIN, HULTA, DE GATIN, VONDERMAN AND CESARIO, THE HORSEMAN, TO RESCUE THEIR LEADER OR SEEK VENGEANCE.

THERE WAS NEVER A MORE UNTIDY HOUSECLEANING!

HAL FOSTER

NEXT WEEK—
FROM FRYING PAN TO FIRE!

Prince Valiant

IN THE DAYS OF KING ARTHUR
BY HAROLD R FOSTER

Synopsis: KNOWING ONLY THAT PRINCE VALIANT, THEIR GAY LEADER, IS PRISONER IN PISCARO'S PALACE, HIS FRIENDS STAKE THEIR LIVES ON A DESPERATE RESCUE.

ROUSED FROM HIS WEARY VIGIL BEFORE THE PALACE GATE, FAITHFUL SLITH SEES THEM COMING AND SNATCHES HIS WEAPONS FROM SOCRATES' PACK.

THE MEMORY OF CRUEL INJUSTICES LENDS STRENGTH TO THE ARMS OF DUKE CESARIO'S KNIGHTS, AS THEY SWEEP PISCARO'S FOLLOWERS FROM THE PALACE.

AS THEY BREAK IN PANIC TOWARD THE GATE, A WILD BATTLE-CRY IS HEARD AND VAL'S FRIENDS COME CRASHING THROUGH.

THE MORNING'S WORK IS SMARTLY FINISHED AND WEEKS OF ANXIETY ARE FORGOTTEN, AS GOOD FRIENDS MEET AGAIN. *"THERE IS NOTHING LIKE A LITTLE EXERCISE BEFORE LUNCH TO GIVE ONE AN APPETITE,"* REMARKS TRISTRAM, LOOKING ANXIOUSLY OVER THE SLAIN TO SEE IF ANY OF THE KITCHEN STAFF HAD BEEN WASTED.

" PISCARO IS SLAIN. DUKE CESARIO REIGNS, WE ARE FREE AGAIN!"

THE HUNS HEAR AND TREMBLE - FOR UNDER PISCARO'S RULE THEY DID AS THEY PLEASED AND HEAPED INSULT AND INDIGNITY UPON THE HELPLESS CITIZENS.

THEN COMES A NIGHT OF HORROR, AS THE MEN OF PANDARIS TURN ON THEIR SNEERING OPPRESSORS AND HUNT THEM THROUGH THE STREETS.

NEXT WEEK—
BACK TO DUTY AND A PLAN.

151 12-31-39   Copr. 1939, King Features Syndicate, Inc., World rights reserved.

HAL FOSTER

FAR EAST
CATHAY
SAVE THIS STAMP

Prince Valiant

IN THE DAYS OF
KING ARTHUR
BY
HAROLD R FOSTER

FAR EAST
MONGOL
SAVE THIS STAMP

Synopsis: PISCARO ORDERS A HORRIBLE DEATH FOR PRINCE VALIANT, BUT IN THE END IS TRICKED INTO CHANGING PLACES WITH HIS INTENDED VICTIM. VAL, ACTING THE PART OF PISCARO, LIBERATES CESARIO, THE REAL DUKE, AND ONCE MORE BEAUTIFUL PANDARIS IS FREED FROM THE HUN.

THE MENACE OF THE HUN HAS LAIN LIKE AN EVIL SHADOW OVER THE CITY, AND THIS NIGHT, WHILE THE NOBLES FEAST, THE PEOPLE HUNT THEIR SAVAGE OPPRESSORS THROUGH THE DARK STREETS. WHEN THE LONG NIGHT OF HORROR ENDS THERE IS NO LIVING HUN WITHIN THE CITY'S GATES.

"YOU HAVE PUT AN END TO A TERRIBLE NIGHTMARE, SIR VALIANT, ASK WHAT YOU WILL OF ME."

VAL LEARNS THAT 4000 HUNS HAVE COME THROUGH THE PANDARIS PASS TO ATTACK HIS ARMY FROM THE REAR. HALF THIS NUMBER HAVE PERISHED DURING THE NIGHT.........

ALL THE BELLS ARE RINGING JOYOUSLY, THERE IS MUSIC IN THE STREETS AND THE PEOPLE ARE DANCING... FREEDOM AND LAUGHTER HAVE COME AGAIN TO PANDARIS! THROUGH THIS BRIGHT SCENE VAL RIDES TO THE GRIM BUSINESS AHEAD.

"LOAN ME 500 HEAVILY ARMED KNIGHTS AND I WILL SWEEP THIS SIDE OF THE MOUNTAINS CLEAR OF HUNS, AND YOU, CESARIO, LET NO MORE THROUGH THE PASS ABOVE PANDARIS."

HAL FOSTER

152 1-7-40

NEXT WEEK—
THE INVINCIBLES FALL!

Prince Valiant

IN THE DAYS OF
KING ARTHUR
BY
HAROLD R FOSTER

MEDIEVAL SADDLE — SAVE THIS STAMP

MEDIEVAL SADDLE — SAVE THIS STAMP

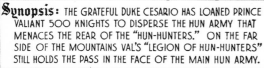

Synopsis: THE GRATEFUL DUKE CESARIO HAS LOANED PRINCE VALIANT 500 KNIGHTS TO DISPERSE THE HUN ARMY THAT MENACES THE REAR OF THE "HUN-HUNTERS." ON THE FAR SIDE OF THE MOUNTAINS VAL'S "LEGION OF HUN-HUNTERS" STILL HOLDS THE PASS IN THE FACE OF THE MAIN HUN ARMY.

TO HIS OFFICERS THE YOUNG PRINCE EXPLAINS HIS PLAN OF ATTACK..... THEY IN TURN FALL BACK AND INSTRUCT THE OTHER KNIGHTS, AS THEY MOVE SWIFTLY FORWARD.

SCOUTS SEE THEM COMING AND SPEED TO THEIR CHIEFTAIN WITH THEIR NEWS.

FOR SIX YEARS THESE BARBARIANS HAVE PILLAGED EUROPE AT WILL WITHOUT DEFEAT --- CONFIDENTLY THEY PREPARE FOR ANOTHER VICTORY.

THE AIR TREMBLES WITH SAVAGE CRIES AND THUNDERING HOOFS, AS THE INVINCIBLE HUN BATTLE FORMATION RUSHES FORWARD, — WINGS WIDE-SPREAD LIKE ENGULFING HORNS.

BUT VAL HAS BEEN SCHOOLED IN BATTLE AT THE COURT OF KING ARTHUR..... AT A COMMAND HIS MAIL-CLAD WARRIORS FORM THE TERRIBLE WEDGE AND CHARGE.

NOTHING HUMAN COULD WITHSTAND THAT IRON-CLAD BLOW. THE HUNS' LEFT WING IS SLICED OFF AND CRUMPLES.

THEN, SWERVING RIGHT AND LEFT THEY SWEEP FURIOUSLY DOWN THE ENEMY LINE.... ROLLING IT BACK IN HELPLESS CONFUSION.

VAL SEEKS AND FINDS THE HUN CHIEFTAIN....SOON THEIR BUSINESS TOGETHER IS FINISHED AND VAL GAZES OVER THE STREWN FIELD. GRIMLY, EFFICIENTLY HIS MEN ARE EXTERMINATING THE FLEEING HUNS.

153 1-14-40

HIGH ON THE PASS THEIR WORK IS COMPLETED AND THEY PART.... VAL AND HIS FRIENDS TO CROSS OVER AND ONCE AGAIN TAKE COMMAND OF THE "LEGION OF HUN-HUNTERS."

NEXT WEEK—
FAMINE

HAL FOSTER

MEDIEVAL SADDLE — SAVE THIS STAMP

Prince Valiant

IN THE DAYS OF KING ARTHUR
BY HAROLD R FOSTER

Synopsis: THREE LONG WEEKS HAVE PASSED SINCE VAL LAST SAW HIS LITTLE "LEGION OF HUN-HUNTERS." IN THE MEANTIME, HE HAS LEARNED ONE GREAT FACT: THE ONCE-INVINCIBLE HUN CAN BE BEATEN!

WHEN THEY COME IN SIGHT OF THE CAMP VAL CRIES OUT IN ASTONISHMENT--- HIS LITTLE BAND HAS GROWN TO AN ARMY, 7000 STRONG.

NEWS OF HIS SUCCESSFUL RAIDS HAS SPREAD THROUGHOUT EUROPE...... THERE COME KNIGHTS ERRANT SEEKING ADVENTURE, BANDITS SEEKING LOOT, DESPOILED NOBLES SEEKING REVENGE AND WARRIORS SEEKING A LEADER WORTH FOLLOWING.

A VAST STORE OF SUPPLIES HAD BEEN TAKEN FROM THE HUNS, BUT HARDLY ENOUGH TO FEED THIS GREAT NUMBER. VAL LEARNS THAT FAMINE IS UPON THEM.

A TERRIBLE RESPONSIBILITY FOR SO YOUNG A LAD – SHOULD HE FAIL TO HOLD THE PASS EUROPE WILL BE AGAIN OVERRUN BY THE HUN.

AT DAWN A PANTING SCOUT ARRIVES, "SIR VALIANT, THE HUNS PREPARE TO ATTACK!"

"OH! FOR A PLAN," CRIES VAL, "A PLAN THAT WILL ENABLE 7000 STARVING CHRISTIANS TO DEFEAT 20,000 HUNS WITH A FORTIFIED CAMP!"

FROM A ROCKY OUTPOST VAL AND SLITH LOOK DOWN ON THE ENEMY CAMP. THERE IS GREAT ACTIVITY AND, THEY JUDGE, THE HUNS WILL MARCH FORTH NEXT DAWN TO SWEEP THE PASS. SUPPLY TRAINS ARE STILL ENTERING THE GATE..... ....."WISH WE COULD ENTER AS EASILY," SAYS SLITH.

"WE CAN!" SHOUTS VAL, "WE WILL!, BY ZEUS, A PLAN! SUMMON THE COUNCIL.... VICTORY MAY YET BE OURS!"

NEXT WEEK—
THE HUNS MARCH.

SPURS
SAVE THIS STAMP

Prince Valiant

IN THE DAYS OF
KING ARTHUR
BY
HAROLD R FOSTER

SPURS
SAVE THIS STAMP

Synopsis: FOR MONTHS PRINCE VALIANT AND HIS COUNCIL HAVE SOUGHT A PLAN WHEREBY THEIR 7000 MEN MIGHT HOPE TO HALT THE 20,000 SAVAGE HUNS SENT TO CLEAR THE PASS AND OPEN THE WAY FOR FURTHER ONSLAUGHTS UPON EUROPE. A CHANCE REMARK OF SLITH'S GIVES VAL AN IDEA.

THE PLAN IS DARING, INSPIRED, DANGEROUS, BUT THEIR DESPERATE PLIGHT CALLS FOR A DESPERATE PLAN, AND VAL'S ENTHUSIASM FINALLY WINS CONSENT FROM THE COUNCIL.

DEFEAT WILL COST HIM HIS HEAD, SO KARNAK, CHIEFTAIN OF THE HUNS, HAS PROCEEDED CAREFULLY. HIS BASE IS FORTIFIED AND PILED HIGH WITH SUPPLIES.... HIS FIERCE WARRIORS ARE CLAMORING TO BE LOOSED UPON THEIR NIMBLE FOES.

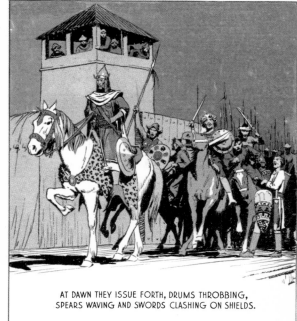

AT DAWN THEY ISSUE FORTH, DRUMS THROBBING, SPEARS WAVING AND SWORDS CLASHING ON SHIELDS.

LIKE A GREAT OCTOPUS THE HUN ARMY MOVES SLOWLY UP THE WIDE VALLEY, ITS FAR-FLUNG ARMS SWEEPING EVERY FOLD AND HOLLOW OF THE ENCIRCLING HILLS.

"GENTLEMEN, THE HUN IS IN FRONT OF US, FAMINE LURKS BEHIND. TO-NIGHT WE BANQUET ROYALLY ON THE LAST OF OUR PROVISIONS..... AND TO-MORROW?.... DEATH OR PLENTY!"

FROM AMONG THE RANKS WILY SLITH CHOOSES ALL THOSE WHO MOST RESEMBLE HUNS, PUTS HUN COSTUMES OVER THEIR ARMOR, THEN, WITH A MYSTERIOUS PACK TRAIN DISAPPEARS SILENTLY INTO THE NIGHT.

HAL FOSTER

BY NOON OF THIS, THE SECOND DAY, KARNAK IS WELL UP THE PASS AND STILL NO SIGN OF AN ENEMY. INDEED, THERE IS NO ENEMY, FOR.........

VAL HAD SAID TO HIS HUN-HUNTERS: "KARNAK'S WOLVES ARE AT THE MOUTH OF OUR CANYON. HULTA WILL LEAD US BY A SECRET WAY TO THE PLAINS BELOW, THERE TO PUT OUR PLAN TO THE TEST."

NEXT WEEK—
VAL INVITES KARNAK TO DINE!

Synopsis: UNDER PRINCE VALIANT'S DARING LEADERSHIP THE "LEGION OF HUN-HUNTERS" HAS RAIDED THE HUNS AGAIN AND AGAIN AND THEIR SUCCESS BROUGHT NEW HOPE TO THE PEOPLE OF EUROPE AND SUCH RAGE TO THE BARBARIANS THAT A GREAT ARMY UNDER "KARNAK, THE FEROCIOUS" HAS BEEN SENT AGAINST THEM.

DUSK OF THE SECOND DAY. HIGH UP NEAR THE TOP OF THE PASS THE HUN ARMY PAUSES..... NO ENEMY HAS YET BEEN SEEN, NOTHING BUT SILENCE AND DESOLATION. AND KARNAK, REMEMBERING THE THREAT OF THE GREAT KAHN, SHUDDERS WITH DREAD.

NO ENEMY OF THE HUN IS ON THAT PASS, FOR, LED BY HULTA DOWN A SECRET WAY, THEY HAVE DESCENDED TO THE PLAIN CLOSE BY THE FORTIFIED CAMP.

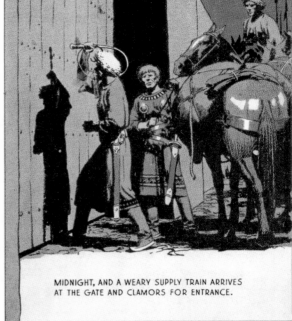

MIDNIGHT, AND A WEARY SUPPLY TRAIN ARRIVES AT THE GATE AND CLAMORS FOR ENTRANCE.

THE GATE SWINGS WIDE AND THROUGH THE GUARDS THE TIRED, TRAVEL-STAINED CARAVAN SLOWLY MAKES ITS WAY. THE GATES ARE SWINGING SHUT WHEN........

.......VAL HAD REMEMBERED THE WOODEN HORSE OF TROY......THE SAME TRICK......UP FROM THE PACK-HORSES LEAP ARMED MEN.....A SHORT SHARP STRUGGLE.....AGAIN THE GATES SWING WIDE—AND....

.....ACROSS THE MOONLIT PLAIN COMES THE SWELLING THUNDER OF GALLOPING HORSES AND THE MOUNTED "HUN-HUNTERS" BURST FURIOUSLY INTO THE SLEEPING CAMP, SHOUTING.

THE IRRESISTIBLE CHARGE OF THE HORSE-MEN SPREADS PANIC EVERYWHERE.....THEN COME THE GRIM, EFFICIENT FOOT SOLDIERS UNDER VONDERMAN AND THE CAMP IS WON.

"YOUR LIFE HAS BEEN SPARED THAT YOU MAY CARRY THIS MESSAGE TO KARNAK."

"FROM MY FORTIFIED BASE CAMP..... AN INVITATION TO DINE, SIGNED BY PRINCE VALIANT." THE FACE OF KARNAK IS WHITE WITH RAGE, AS HE DRAWS HIS SWORD AND SLAYS THE MESSENGER

NEXT WEEK—
ODDS OF THREE TO ONE

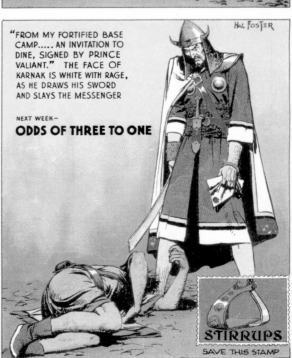

500 AD
SAVE THIS STAMP

Prince Valiant

IN THE DAYS OF
KING ARTHUR
BY
HAROLD R FOSTER

1140
SAVE THIS STAMP

Synopsis: WHEN 'KARNAK, THE FEROCIOUS', LED HIS HUN ARMY AGAINST THE 'LEGION OF HUN-HUNTERS' THAT ELUSIVE BAND SLIPPED BEHIND HIM AND CAPTURED HIS FORTIFIED SUPPLY BASE, LEAVING HIS ARMY WITHOUT FOOD IN THE BARREN MOUNTAINS.

THE CHEERY INVITATION FROM PRINCE VALIANT TO DINE IN HIS OWN CAMP IS AN INSULT THAT DRIVES KARNAK MAD WITH RAGE.

IT IS NOT LONG UNTIL THE WATCHERS ON THE PARAPET SEE THE VAST ARMY COME SWARMING DOWN THE PASS AND FORM ON THE PLAIN BEFORE THE CAMP.

"TO YOUR STATIONS, COMRADES, THERE WILL BE A LIVELY PARTY .....THEY OUTNUMBER US THREE TO ONE..... GOOD LUCK ALL!"

KARNAK DRIVES HIS MEN MERCILESSLY... AGAIN AND AGAIN THEY STORM UP THE EARTHWORKS ONLY TO BE THROWN BACK. AT LAST NIGHT PUTS AN END TO THAT TERRIBLE DAY AND THE EXHAUSTED LIVING DROP TO REST BESIDE THE PEACEFUL DEAD.

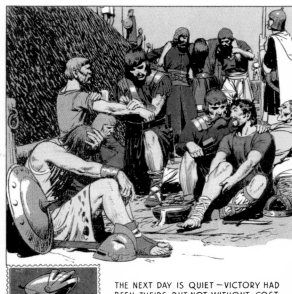

THE NEXT DAY IS QUIET — VICTORY HAD BEEN THEIRS, BUT NOT WITHOUT COST. THE SILENCE OF THE HUNS OUTSIDE IS LIKE AN UNSPOKEN THREAT.

"THE NEXT ATTACK WILL BE BY STARVING, DESPERATE MEN, MEN MAD WITH HUNGER.....OUR DEFENDERS ARE TOO FEW TO GUARANTEE ANOTHER VICTORY..." VAL HESITATES, THEN, HIS FACE ALIGHT WITH ENTHUSIASM, HE UNFOLDS ANOTHER AUDACIOUS PLAN!

157 2-11-40   Copr. 1940, King Features Syndicate, Inc., World rights reserved.

HAL FOSTER

IN THE EARLY DAWN THE "HUN-HUNTERS" MARCH OUT AND FORM IN BATTLE ARRAY .....AND THE DESPAIRING KARNAK ROARS FOR JOY;— FOR YEARS HIS HUNS HAVE BEEN INVINCIBLE IN OPEN BATTLE!

NEXT WEEK— **VAL RETREATS, FOR A REASON!**

1918
SAVE THIS STAMP

TILTING HELM
1000 AD
SAVE THIS STAMP

Prince Valiant

IN THE DAYS OF KING ARTHUR
BY HAROLD R FOSTER

TILTING HELMET
1350 AD
SAVE THIS STAMP

Synopsis: AS USUAL, THE "LEGION OF HUN-HUNTERS" UNDER PRINCE VALIANT'S LEADERSHIP, HAS AVOIDED BATTLE WITH SUPERIOR FORCES AND STRUCK AT THE WEAKEST SPOT, THE SUPPLY BASE. "KARNAK, THE FEROCIOUS", IS PREPARING FOR AN ASSAULT WHEN THE "HUN-HUNTERS" ISSUE FORTH IN BATTLE FORMATION.

FOR THE FIRST TIME KARNAK BEHOLDS HIS ENEMY AND IS AMAZED TO SEE HOW FEW THEY ARE. THE HUNS FORM THEIR BATTLE-LINE AND BOTH SIDES CHARGE!

KARNAK SHOUTS FOR JOY, AS HIS INVINCIBLE HUNS SWEEP DOWN ON THE SCANTY, RAGGED LINE OF HUN-HUNTERS, MOST OF WHOM ARE UNMOUNTED!

AT THE FIRST SHOCK THE HUN-HUNTERS WHEEL THEIR HORSES AND FLY FROM THE FIELD IN PANIC.......

AND THE HUNS, MOST FEROCIOUS WARRIORS THE WORLD HAS EVER SEEN, ARE UNLEASHED IN A SCREAMING MOB UPON THE FLEEING ENEMY!

SUDDENLY, THROUGH THE DUST OF THEIR RETREATING COMRADES, APPEAR THE FORGOTTEN FOOT-SOLDIERS BEHIND A GLEAMING WALL OF SPEARS AND SHARPENED STAKES AND THE FRONT LINE OF HUNS GOES DOWN BEFORE A HISSING CLOUD OF ARROWS!

FOR A MOMENT THE WILD RUSH IS HALTED, CONFUSED;— THEN, FROM A HIDDEN GULLEY COMES THE FULL FORCE OF VAL'S MOUNTED TROOPS AT A GALLOP.

NOTE:— IT IS A CURIOUS FACT THAT THE STRATEGY OF A KNIGHT OF KING ARTHUR'S ROUND TABLE, PRINCE VALIANT, SHOULD HAVE CAUSED THE DOWNFALL OF BRITAIN.... FOR IN 1066, WILLIAM, THE CONQUEROR, USED THIS SAME PLAN AT THE BATTLE OF HASTINGS AND ALL ENGLAND FELL TO THE NORMANS

HAL FOSTER

PRINCE VALIANT'S STRATEGY IS SUCCESSFUL; THE HUN BATTLE FORMATION HAS BROKEN, THE FOOT SOLDIERS HAD MOMENTARILY CONFUSED THEM; THEN, INTO THE BEWILDERED MASS THE TERRIBLE, ARMORED WEDGE CLEAVES LIKE A PLOWSHARE!

NEXT WEEK— **MEDIEVAL PEACE TREATY!**

GLADIATOR HELMET
SAVE THIS STAMP

Prince Valiant

IN THE DAYS OF KING ARTHUR
BY
HAROLD R FOSTER

GLADIATOR HELMET
SAVE THIS STAMP

Synopsis: VICTORY! THE CONFUSED AND BROKEN RANKS OF THE HUN ARMY HAVE FLED WILDLY WITH THE GRIM VICTORS IN MERCILESS PURSUIT. PRINCE VALIANT WATCHES WEARILY; HIS PART IS ACCOMPLISHED; HE HAS SHOWN THE WORLD THAT THE HUN IS NOT INVINCIBLE.

THE STRATEGY, THE CRASH OF BATTLE, A BRAVE HARD-FIGHTING ENEMY AND THEN VICTORY; THESE THINGS ARE THE BREATH OF LIFE TO A WARRIOR! BUT VAL SICKENS AT THE TERRIBLE SLAUGHTER THAT FOLLOWS THESE MEDIEVAL BATTLES

AS HE RIDES SLOWLY BACK TO CAMP HE HEARS A SMALL VOICE CALLING HIM. HE HALTS AND THERE, PINNED TO A SADDLE WITH A CRUEL, BARBED ARROW, IS HULTA, THE MESSENGER.

GENTLY HE WORKS THE ARROW LOOSE FROM THE SADDLE. HULTA SWOONS.

TAKING THE SLENDER FIGURE IN HIS ARMS VAL REPROACHES HIMSELF: "TO THINK I HAVE SENT HIM WITH MESSAGES TO MY OFFICERS IN THE THICK OF EVERY FIGHT AND HE IS ONLY A BOY!"

THE WOUND IS NOT SERIOUS; VAL CUTS THE UGLY BARBED HEAD FROM THE ARROW AND WITHDRAWS THE SHAFT.

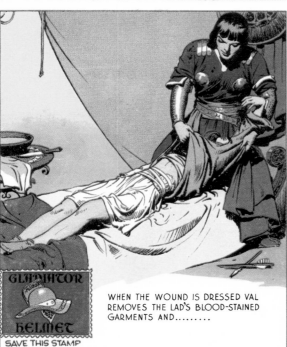

WHEN THE WOUND IS DRESSED VAL REMOVES THE LAD'S BLOOD-STAINED GARMENTS AND.........

GREAT GLEAMING COILS OF COPPER-COLORED HAIR SPREAD SLOWLY OVER THE PILLOW LIKE BRIGHT SERPENTS....... HULTA IS A GIRL!

NEXT WEEK— **A GIRL AND A PROPHECY!**

Hal Foster

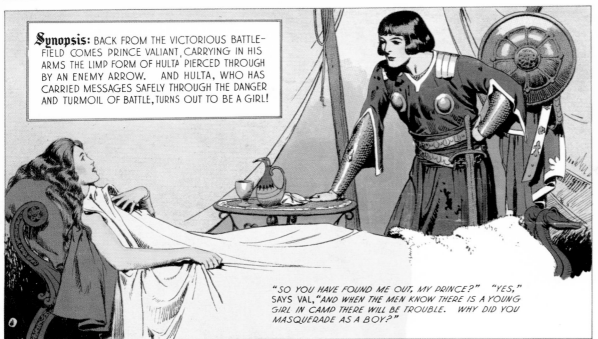

Synopsis: BACK FROM THE VICTORIOUS BATTLE-FIELD COMES PRINCE VALIANT, CARRYING IN HIS ARMS THE LIMP FORM OF HULTA PIERCED THROUGH BY AN ENEMY ARROW. AND HULTA, WHO HAS CARRIED MESSAGES SAFELY THROUGH THE DANGER AND TURMOIL OF BATTLE, TURNS OUT TO BE A GIRL!

"SO YOU HAVE FOUND ME OUT, MY PRINCE?" "YES," SAYS VAL, "AND WHEN THE MEN KNOW THERE IS A YOUNG GIRL IN CAMP THERE WILL BE TROUBLE. WHY DID YOU MASQUERADE AS A BOY?"

"MY FATHER WAS A CHIEFTAIN OF THE SHEPHERD TRIBES HEREABOUT. THE HUNS CAME.....ONLY I ESCAPED. EVEN WOMEN MUST FIGHT NOW-A-DAYS AND I AM A WARRIOR'S DAUGHTER."

"......AND ANOTHER WORRY FOR ME," ADDS VAL. "OH! WELL, I'LL EVEN MATTERS UP BY PASSING ON A WORRY TO KALLA KHAN." AND HE SENDS FOR TWO HUN PRISONERS AND THE BODY OF "KARNAK, THE FEROCIOUS".

AND KALLA KHAN IS NOT OVERLY PLEASED WITH THE GHASTLY PRESENT NOR THE MESSAGE WHICH READS, "YOU PROMISED TO CUT OFF THE HEAD OF 'KARNAK, THE FEROCIOUS' SHOULD HE FAIL. I HAVE COURTEOUSLY SAVED YOU THIS TROUBLE; IT WAS A PLEASURE. MANY MORE OF YOUR GENERALS WILL FAIL AND ADD THEIR HEADS TO YOUR COLLECTION FOR I HAVE SHOWN THE WORLD THE HUNS ARE NOT INVINCIBLE. THE HUNS ALSO KNOW THIS AND THEIR POWER IS GONE FOREVER." AND IN HIS HEART KALLA KHAN KNOWS THIS TO BE TRUE.

HAL FOSTER

"DELIVER THIS MESSAGE AND THIS CASKET TO KALLA KHAN OF THE HUNS AND," HE ADDS OMINOUSLY, "IT IS BETTER NOT TO FAIL."

NEXT WEEK— **GIRL TROUBLE.**

160 3-3-40 Copr. 1940, King Features Syndicate, Inc., World rights reserved.

WILLIAM A.D. 1066 THE CONQUERER SAVE THIS STAMP

ANCIENT GREEK
SAVE THIS STAMP

TROJAN
SAVE THIS STAMP

Synopsis: CALLING HIS COUNCIL TOGETHER, PRINCE VALIANT SPEAKS AS FOLLOWS: *FOR ME THIS WAR AND ITS CARES AND WORRIES ARE ENDED. YOU, PISCARO, HUNT DOWN ALL THE REMAINING HUNS WITHOUT MERCY; VONDERMAN, FORTIFY THE PASS. TRISTRAM, ESTABLISH A FORM OF GOVERNMENT; DE GATIN, DIVIDE THE LAND AMONG THE WARRIORS. SLITH, YOU DIVIDE THE LOOT ACCORDING TO RANK. AND YOU, GAWAIN, MY OLD MASTER, PLEASE STAY OUT OF TROUBLE FOR YET A LITTLE WHILE!"*

"AND HULTA, IT SEEMS, IS A GIRL. SHE IS UNDER MY PROTECTION; WHO HARMS HER MUST ANSWER TO ME."

HULTA, GRACEFUL AND HEALTHY AS A YOUNG ANIMAL, SOON RECOVERS FROM HER WOUND. EVERYONE AGREES THAT SHE GIVES A DECORATIVE TOUCH TO THE CAMP.

NO ONE ADMIRES HER MORE THAN SLITH, WHO, REMEMBERING THAT HE HAD BEEN HER CHOSEN FRIEND WHEN SHE WAS MASQUERADING AS A BOY, THINKS...... WELL......

KNOWING SHE IS ALONE IN HER TENT HE MAKES BOLD TO ENTER......

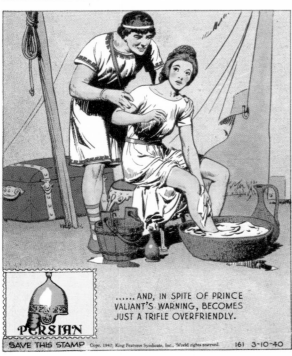

......AND, IN SPITE OF PRINCE VALIANT'S WARNING, BECOMES JUST A TRIFLE OVERFRIENDLY.

HEARING A CRASH AND A YELL FROM HULTA'S TENT VAL RUNS TO INVESTIGATE AND FINDS THE GIRL WEEPING OVER THE UNCONSCIOUS SLITH! *"OH! I HAVE HURT THE POOR BOY!"*

HAL FOSTER

"I'VE LOVED THIS POOR, SHREWD LITTLE GREEK CLOWN FROM THE FIRST", SHE EXPLAINS, "I JUST CAN'T HELP IT!"

NEXT WEEK—
A KINGDOM IS FOUNDED.

PERSIAN
SAVE THIS STAMP

BABYLONIAN
SAVE THIS STAMP

VIKING RAVEN
SAVE THIS STAMP

Prince Valiant

IN THE DAYS OF KING ARTHUR
BY
Harold R. Foster

DRAGON OF CATHAY
SAVE THIS STAMP

Synopsis: SLITH, ONE-TIME THIEF, IS A VERY CLEVER LAD; IN FACT, TOO CLEVER FOR HIS OWN GOOD, AND WHEN HULTA TURNS OUT TO BE NOT AN AGILE BOY, BUT A SPLENDID, TALL GIRL, SHE HAS TO BREAK AN OAKEN WATER BUCKET ON HIS HEAD IN ORDER TO TEACH HIM RESPECT FOR A HELPLESS MAID !

"SO, HULTA, YOU LOVE THE LITTLE RASCAL ? I DON'T SEE HOW HE CAN LONG WITHSTAND THE ARDOR OF YOUR WOOING," LAUGHS VAL.

BESIDE A COOL SPRING SLITH BATHES HIS BATTERED BROW. HIS RESPECT FOR HULTA IS AS GREAT AS THE ACHE IN HIS HEAD, WHICH IS CONSIDERABLE. A WARRIOR'S DAUGHTER, HE REFLECTS, IS TOO HIGH-SPIRITED FOR HIM !

WHILE THE WARRIOR'S DAUGHTER WEEPS LIKE ANY OTHER YOUNG GIRL, THINKING SHE HAS SLAIN CUPID WITH A WATER BUCKET.

MEANWHILE, A PROBLEM CONFRONTS THE COUNCIL: A LARGE TERRITORY HAS BEEN RE-CAPTURED, FORTIFIED AND A SYSTEM OF GOVERNMENT INSTALLED, BUT NO RULER CAN BE FOUND. WITH THE WAR AT AN END ALL THE OFFICERS LONG FOR THEIR DISTANT HOMES AGAIN. QUIETLY HULTA LEAVES THE COUNCIL.

WITHIN HER TENT SHE UNPACKS THE GREAT SWORD AND SHIELD HER FATHER HAD CARRIED WHEN, IN HAPPIER TIMES, HE HAD RULED THE SHEPHERD TRIBES HEREABOUTS.

SLOWLY SHE WALKS THROUGH THE CAMP CHANTING AN ANCIENT BATTLE HYMN AND THE WARRIORS OF HER TRIBE, RECOGNIZING THEIR CHIEFTAIN'S DAUGHTER, FOLLOW.

162. 3.17.40.

BEFORE THE COUNCIL PAVILION SHE HALTS "MY FATHER RULED ALL THESE LANDS BEFORE THE COMING OF THE HUNS - I AM HIS DAUGHTER. CAN YOU FIND A BETTER RULER ?"

HAL FOSTER

NEXT WEEK - **A Rival !**

Synopsis: AFTER THEIR SMASHING VICTORY THE "LEGION OF HUN-HUNTERS" HAVE IN THEIR POSSESSION THE PASS, ITS RICH GRAZING LANDS AND FERTILE VALLEYS. SO FAR NO ONE HAS BEEN CHOSEN AS RULER OF THIS TERRITORY. ALONE IN HER TENT HULTA BUCKLES AROUND HER SLIM WAIST THE GREAT SWORD HER FATHER HAD CARRIED AS HE RAGED TO AND FRO ACROSS SO MANY BATTLEFIELDS, AND, CARRYING HIS BATTERED SHIELD, WALKS SLOWLY THROUGH THE CAMP. THE WARRIORS OF HER TRIBE FOLLOW CURIOUSLY.

"MY FATHER RULED ALL THE LANDS HEREABOUT BEFORE THE COMING OF THE HUN.....THESE ARE WARRIORS WHO HAVE FOLLOWED THIS SWORD AND THIS SHIELD......THEY WILL STILL FOLLOW THEM. I WILL RULE THE LAND!"

FOR A LONG MOMENT VAL GAZES INTO THE CALM, FEARLESS EYES OF THIS TALL GIRL. "BY THE GODS I BELIEVE YOU ARE THE ONE TO DO IT!" HE EXCLAIMS.

"WHAT IS THE CAUSE OF ALL THIS MISERY, SLITH?"
"HULTA....SHE IS A GODDESS, NEVER HAVE I KNOWN A LOVELIER GIRL, BUT, ALAS! SHE IS TOO FAR ABOVE ME NOW!"
"I HAVE REASON TO BELIEVE SHE WILL LISTEN TO WHATEVER YOU MAY HAVE TO SAY," HINTS VAL.

HOPEFULLY, SLITH GOES IN SEARCH OF HULTA AND FINDS HER RETURNING FROM A BEAR HUNT.

"STAY A WHILE, HULTA, THERE IS SOMETHING I MUST TELL YOU AND A QUESTION I MUST ASK."

LEAPING LIGHTLY DOWN FROM THE HALF-WILD STALLION SHE HAS BEEN RIDING AND SENDING THE HARD-RIDING ESCORT ON WITH THE BEAR SHE HAS JUST SLAIN, HULTA TIMIDLY SAYS "YES" TO SLITH'S QUESTION.
163 3-24.40.

JOYOUSLY THE TWO LOVERS RIDE BACK TO CAMP; FOR SLITH TRULY LOVES THIS SPLENDID GIRL NOW THAT SHE IS CHIEFTAIN OF A RICH LAND AND IS VERY, VERY WEALTHY!

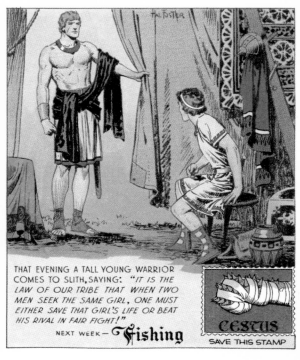

THAT EVENING A TALL YOUNG WARRIOR COMES TO SLITH, SAYING: "IT IS THE LAW OF OUR TRIBE THAT WHEN TWO MEN SEEK THE SAME GIRL, ONE MUST EITHER SAVE THAT GIRL'S LIFE OR BEAT HIS RIVAL IN FAIR FIGHT!"
NEXT WEEK— **Fishing**

Synopsis: SLITH REALLY LOVES HULTA IN HIS SHREWD AND SUBTLE WAY, AND, WHEN SHE BECOMES RULER OF A RICH LAND, HIS LOVE INCREASES WITH HER WEALTH. BUT TO WIN HER HE HAS EITHER TO SAVE HER LIFE OR FIGHT ALL RIVALS. AND HULTA, A CHIEFTAIN'S DAUGHTER, IS WELL ABLE TO TAKE CARE OF HERSELF IN ANY DANGER AND HIS ONE RIVAL IS A STALWART YOUNG WARRIOR.

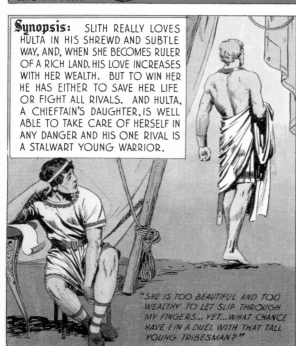

"SHE IS TOO BEAUTIFUL AND TOO WEALTHY TO LET SLIP THROUGH MY FINGERS... YET... WHAT CHANCE HAVE I IN A DUEL WITH THAT TALL YOUNG TRIBESMAN?"

FEELING THE NEED OF ADVICE, SYMPATHY AND HELP HE GOES TO PRINCE VALIANT'S TENT ONLY TO FIND THAT VAL HAD LEFT CAMP AT DAWN, ALONE.

FOR DAYS HE HAD BEEN BUSY WITH LANCEWOOD AND THREAD, COLORED FEATHERS, GLUE, HOOKS, HORSEHAIR AND LINE. NOW HE IS OFF TO THE CLEAR MOUNTAIN STREAMS FOR A FEW DAYS SPORT.

FOR VAL GREW UP IN SPORT-LOVING ENGLAND AND A FEW DAYS ON THE TROUT STREAMS BACK AMONG THE HILLS IS NOT TO BE MISSED.

DEEP IN THE FOREST VAL LETS THE LONELY MUSIC OF WIND IN THE TREE-TOPS AND THE MERRY SONG OF RUNNING WATER SOOTHE AWAY THE CARES AND ANXIETIES OF HIS GREAT CAMPAIGN.

BUT THE STORY OF THAT VICTORY SPREAD FAR AND WIDE AND KINGS AND RULERS ALL ACROSS THE LAND SEND ENVOYS, EACH BEARING THE SAME MESSAGE.

DURING VAL'S ABSENCE THEY COME, AND RICH AND MAGNIFICENT ARE THESE NOBLE EMISSARIES WITH THEIR GLITTERING RETINUES.

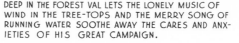

164 3-31-40

"OUR ROYAL MASTERS HAVE SENT US TO OFFER YOUR ABSENT LEADER OUR WEALTH, OUR ARMIES, OUR LIVES, IF HE WILL LEAD US INTO PANNONIA AND ONCE AND FOR ALL CRUSH THE HUN NATION..... ONLY PRINCE VALIANT CAN DO THIS SUCCESSFULLY!"

NEXT WEEK— **The Answer**

Prince Valiant

IN THE DAYS OF
KING ARTHUR
BY
HAROLD R FOSTER

Synopsis: NEWS OF PRINCE VALIANT'S SUCCESSFUL CAMPAIGN AGAINST THE HUNS SPREAD QUICKLY AND FROM FAR AND WIDE COME THE ENVOYS OF KINGS OFFERING THEIR ARMIES FOR THE YOUNG PRINCE TO LEAD IN A WAR OF EXTERMINATION AGAINST THE HATED HUNS.

"THE MIGHTY PRINCE VALIANT WILL LEAD US ACROSS PANNONIA THROUGH A SEA OF HUNNISH BLOOD.... LIKE ALEXANDER, THE GREAT, HE INSPIRES A CERTAINTY OF VICTORY.... HIS BRILLIANT TACTICS RIVAL THE GREAT CAESAR, HIMSELF......

"PARDON, SIR, BUT HERE COMES OUR MIGHTY CHIEFTAIN NOW!" AND ENTERS, NOT A STERN GENERAL IN SHINING ARMOR, BUT A DISHEVELED, SUN-BRONZED LAD CARRYING A STRING OF FISH.

THE DIGNIFIED AMBASSADORS FROWN ANGRILY, FOR THEY THINK THIS AN ILL-TIMED JOKE.

BUT WHEN THE LAD SPEAKS IT IS WITH THE CONFIDENCE AND COURTESY THAT BEFIT A PRINCE. "NOW, GENTLEMEN, I KNOW YOUR MISSION I ALSO KNOW THAT WARS OF AGGRESSION ARE BUT BREEDERS OF FUTURE WARS."

"HERE, UNDER MY HAND, IS THE HISTORY OF THE WORLD. NOWHERE CAN I FIND A LASTING CONQUEST BY FORCE. ALEXANDER AND CAESAR IN TURN CONQUERED THE WORLD BUT WHERE ARE THEIR CONQUESTS NOW? WHAT OF BABYLON, OF PERSIA, OF CARTHAGE? THE FRUITS OF CONQUEST ARE BUT SULLEN ENMITIES. NO, NOBLE SIRS, I HAVE PLEDGED MY SWORD IN THE CAUSE OF JUSTICE AND FREEDOM ONLY!"

NEXT WEEK—
Slith's Cowardice.

165 4-7-40   Copr. 1940, King Features Syndicate, Inc., World rights reserved

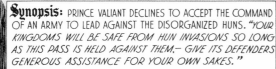

Synopsis: PRINCE VALIANT DECLINES TO ACCEPT THE COMMAND OF AN ARMY TO LEAD AGAINST THE DISORGANIZED HUNS. "YOUR KINGDOMS WILL BE SAFE FROM HUN INVASIONS SO LONG AS THIS PASS IS HELD AGAINST THEM.— GIVE ITS DEFENDERS GENEROUS ASSISTANCE FOR YOUR OWN SAKES."

"THIS IS HULTA, CHIEFTAINESS OF THE DEFENDERS OF THE PASS."

HULTA ESCORTS THE AMBASSADORS OVER THE PASS WHERE A STRONGLY FORTIFIED CITY IS RAPIDLY TAKING FORM.

THEN COMES THE TASK OF ESTABLISHING THE BORDERS AND ALLOTTING THE LAND. HAPPY DAYS FOR SLITH, FOR HE AND HULTA ARE MUCH TOGETHER.

HIS HAPPINESS WOULD BE COMPLETE WERE IT NOT FOR THAT TRIBAL CUSTOM; THAT HE MUST FIGHT ALL RIVALS TO PROVE HIMSELF WORTHY

BANDS OF STARVING HUNS, FUGITIVES FROM THE DEFEATED ARMY, STILL INFEST THE HILLS.... SUCH A GANG HAS FOLLOWED THE PARTY FOR DAYS, SEEKING PLUNDER.

AT DAWN HULTA GOES TO BATHE IN A POOL FAR FROM THE CAMP. THE WATCHFUL HUNS CREEP CLOSER, GRINNING.

ABOVE THE MURMUR OF THE STREAM SLITH HEARS A MUFFLED SCREAM AND CRUEL LAUGHTER.

RUNNING SWIFTLY TOWARD THE SOUND, SLITH SEES HIS BELOVED HULTA STRUGGLING IN THE GRASP OF FIVE ARMED HUNS!

SLITH PAUSES — HE LOVES THIS TAWNY GIRL, AND HER GREAT FORTUNE ALSO......BUT HE IS UNARMED, ONE AGAINST FIVE........ONE MUST BE LOGICAL ABOVE ALL ELSE, HE REFLECTS, STILL HESITATING,......

NEXT WEEK - **Madness!**

HAL FOSTER

Prince Valiant

IN THE DAYS OF KING ARTHUR
BY HAROLD R FOSTER

Synopsis: A BAND OF FUGITIVE HUNS COMES UPON HULTA BATHING SOME DISTANCE FROM THE CAMP. SLITH ARRIVES ON THE SCENE, UNARMED SAVE FOR HIS SLING AND SEES THE GIRL HE LOVES BEING TAKEN FROM HIM. LIFE IS SWEET, HE REFLECTS, EVEN WITHOUT HER AND HER GREAT WEALTH, WHY RISK IT?

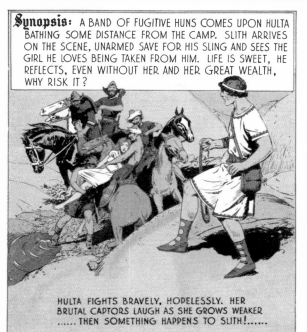

HULTA FIGHTS BRAVELY, HOPELESSLY. HER BRUTAL CAPTORS LAUGH AS SHE GROWS WEAKER ...... THEN SOMETHING HAPPENS TO SLITH!......

...... HE GOES MAD, QUITE MAD! FORGOTTEN IS HIS SHREWDNESS, THE DANGER, THE ODDS AGAINST HIM....THE GIRL HE LOVES IS IN PERIL!

THEY SEE HIM COMING AND ONE GRINNING HUN PREPARES TO CUT DOWN THE RECKLESS, UNARMED FOOL.

BUT A SLING IS A TERRIBLE WEAPON IN THE HANDS OF AN EXPERT.......

.......AND EVEN IN HIS FRANTIC ANGER SLITH IS STILL AN EXPERT.

ANOTHER OF THE HUNS MAKES THE MISTAKE OF FORGETTING THEIR VICTIM IS A WARRIOR'S DAUGHTER.

AND AGAIN THE LOADED SLING DOES ITS WORK.

IT ALL HAPPENED SO QUICKLY THAT, BEFORE THE REMAINING HUNS CAN STRING THEIR BOWS, SLITH AND HULTA ARE RUNNING TOWARD THE RIVER.

167 4-21-40   Copr. 1940, King Features Syndicate, Inc., World rights reserved

AS THEY PLUNGE IN SLITH HEARS HULTA CRY...."I CAN'T SWIM!"

NEXT WEEK — **Targets!**

Synopsis: ALL HIS LIFE SLITH HAS LIVED BY SHREWDNESS AND CUNNING, BUT WHEN HULTA FALLS INTO THE CRUEL HANDS OF A BAND OF HUNS HE DOES A BRAVE, MAD, FOOLISH DEED.

THEY ARE INTO THE SWIRLING RIVER BEFORE SLITH REALIZES THAT HULTA CANNOT SWIM. NO TIME FOR GALLANTRY NOW, HE TAKES A FIRM GRASP ON HER LONG HAIR AND STRIKES OUT STRONGLY.

A ROCK IN MIDSTREAM OFFERS A TEMPORARY SHELTER FROM THE HISSING ARROWS.

THE SOUND OF SLITH'S SHOUTS COMES FAINTLY BACK TO CAMP.

JUST AS THE CLUTCHING WATERS DRAG THEM FROM THEIR HAVEN, HELP ARRIVES.

SWINGING DOWN WITH THE CURRENT SLITH REACHES SHORE WITH HIS FAIR BURDEN.

SUDDENLY HE REALIZES THAT THIS TAWNY GIRL IS MORE PRECIOUS TO HIM THAN LIFE ITSELF..... IT FRIGHTENS HIM A LITTLE.

TO THE TRIBESMEN HE CALMLY SAYS; "I INTEND TO MARRY YOUR CHIEFTAIN AND I AM READY TO FIGHT ALL RIVALS AS IS THE CUSTOM!"

"YOU HAVE FULFILLED THE LAW — YOU HAVE SAVED HER LIFE. LET ME BE THE FIRST TO HAIL OUR NEW CHIEF."

16B 4-28-40   Copr. 1940, King Features Syndicate, Inc., World rights reserved.

ALL THIS IS TOO MUCH FOR SLITH...... HE SITS DOWN. AS HE FEELS HER GENTLE ARMS AROUND HIM HE REFLECTS......"NOT ALL MY TRICKERY NOR ALL MY CLEVERNESS HAS BROUGHT ME SUCH SWEET REWARD AS THIS ONE DEED OF HEROISM!"

NEXT WEEK— **Farewell.**

HAL FOSTER

Prince Valiant

IN THE DAYS OF KING ARTHUR
BY
HAROLD R FOSTER

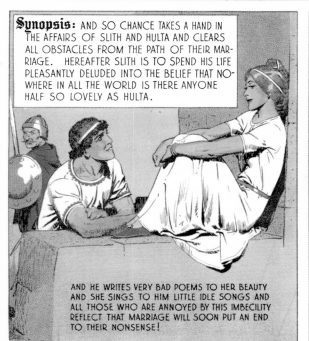

Synopsis: AND SO CHANCE TAKES A HAND IN THE AFFAIRS OF SLITH AND HULTA AND CLEARS ALL OBSTACLES FROM THE PATH OF THEIR MARRIAGE. HEREAFTER SLITH IS TO SPEND HIS LIFE PLEASANTLY DELUDED INTO THE BELIEF THAT NOWHERE IN ALL THE WORLD IS THERE ANYONE HALF SO LOVELY AS HULTA.

AND HE WRITES VERY BAD POEMS TO HER BEAUTY AND SHE SINGS TO HIM LITTLE IDLE SONGS AND ALL THOSE WHO ARE ANNOYED BY THIS IMBECILITY REFLECT THAT MARRIAGE WILL SOON PUT AN END TO THEIR NONSENSE!

AWAY FROM HIS LOVED ONE SLITH IS PRACTICALLY SANE AND TAKES AN ACTIVE PART IN PLANNING THE DEFENSES OF THE PASS.

THE CAPTURED BASE-CAMP IS NOW ALMOST DESERTED. THE WARRIORS, MADE WEALTHY BY THEIR SHARE OF THE SPOILS OF WAR, HAVE GONE THEIR WAY, MOST OF THEM TO TAKE SERVICE UNDER SLITH AND HULTA AND JOIN THEIR TRIBE.

THEIR LAST BANQUET, IN HONOR OF THE MARRIAGE OF SLITH AND HULTA, IS A GAY AFFAIR WITH MUCH SONG AND JEST, LAUGHTER AND SUDDEN SILENCES. FOR THERE ARE HEAVY HEARTS BENEATH ALL THE GAIETY. OLD FRIENDS ARE PARTING AND THEY REMEMBER SHARED DANGERS AND SPLENDID DEEDS IN THE TIME THEY FOUGHT SO DESPERATELY TOGETHER. THE HOUR OF PARTING IS LIKE AN APPROACHING CLOUD.

BUT THE THREE KNIGHTS OF KING ARTHUR'S ROUND TABLE CANNOT BEAR TO PART FOR YET A LITTLE WHILE. THEY SET OUT FOR THE ETERNAL CITY, ROME.

BUT FATE HAS PLACED IN THEIR PATH CERTAIN GAMBLERS, A HATCHET AND A GIANT. THERE WILL BE DELAYS.

NEXT WEEK— **The Gamblers**

169 5-5-40

Prince Valiant

Synopsis: PRINCE VALIANT HAS DONE MORE THAN SHATTER ONE HUN ARMY.... HE HAS DESTROYED THE CONFIDENCE OF A WHOLE NATION IN THEIR INVINCIBILITY. THEY BECOME NOTHING MORE THAN PETTY RAIDERS. NOW, THEIR WORK DONE, TRISTRAN, PRINCE VALIANT AND SIR GAWAIN SET OUT FOR ROME.

AT SUNSET THEY COME TO A SNUG VILLAGE......

AND STOP FOR THE NIGHT AT THE TAVERN.

THERE ARE THREE OTHER GUESTS, GAY YOUNG NOBLES WHO WHILE AWAY THE EVENING HOURS AT DICE. AS THE GAME PROGRESSES THE STAKES BECOME HIGHER....

...... AND SIR GAWAIN, EVER HUNGRY FOR EXCITEMENT JOINS THE GAMESTERS AND THE PLAY THEN BECOMES EARNEST.

DURING THE TIME THEY HAD WANDERED TOGETHER SLITH HAD SHOWN VAL MANY OF HIS SLY TRICKS, SOME OF WHICH, HE NOTICES, ARE USED BY THE BOGUS NOBLES AT THE GAMING TABLE.

BEFORE RETIRING FOR THE NIGHT VAL INSTRUCTS THE STABLE BOY TO CALL HIM IF THE THREE GAMBLERS SHOULD CALL FOR THEIR HORSES.

IN THE EARLY DAWN THE BOY WHISPERS, *"THEY HAVE ORDERED THEIR HORSES SADDLED, SIR, AND WILL LEAVE IN A FEW MINUTES!"*......

......FOR THE GAME HAS ENDED AND SIR GAWAIN IS ADDRESSING SIR GAWAIN *"YOU ARE SIR, WITH MY COMPLIMENTS, A FOOL. I SUSPECT YOU OF BEING TOO STUPID TO LEARN A LESSON. LOSING ALL YOUR MONEY WAS BAD BUT STAKING YOUR HORSE AND GEAR WAS SHEER IDIOCY. I LOOK TO YOUR FUTURE WITH GRAVE MISGIVING!"*

170 5-12-40

THERE IS AN OMINOUS FOREBODING ABOUT THE TWO MAILED FIGURES WHO SILENTLY BAR THE GAMBLERS' DEPARTURE.

NEXT WEEK — **Gawain Turns Turtle.**

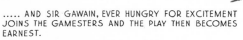

Prince Valiant

IN THE DAYS OF KING ARTHUR
BY
HAROLD R FOSTER

Synopsis: THE THREE KNIGHTS OF THE ROUND TABLE, TRISTRAM, PRINCE VALIANT AND GAWAIN, STOP FOR THE NIGHT AT A TAVERN WHERE THREE GAMBLERS, MASQUERADING AS NOBLEMEN, ENTICE SIR GAWAIN INTO A GAME OF CHANCE AND FLEECE HIM.

WITHOUT A WORD BEING SPOKEN TRISTRAM AND VAL PROD THE BOGUS NOBLES BACK TO THE INN YARD AND CALL SIR GAWAIN.

"GAWAIN, DEAR CHILD, COME....SEE ME WIN BACK YOUR LOSSES. YOU ARE LUCKY THESE BAD MEN DIDN'T TAKE AWAY YOUR TOYS AND SWADDLING CLOTHES, TOO!"

"NOW, MY OILY FRIENDS, WAGER YOUR PURSES AGAINST MINE AND I WILL THROW YOUR DICE AS MY TRICKY FRIEND, SLITH, ONCE SHOWED ME....AND AS YOU DID LAST NIGHT. BEHOLD! I WIN!"

"THE CHEATS!" ROARS THE ANGRY GAWAIN. "I'LL HAVE THEIR HEARTS' BLOOD FOR THAT!" AND STEPS BACK TO WHIP OUT HIS SWORD.........

HE SAID LATER THAT NEVER AGAIN WOULD HE DRAW HIS SWORD IN AN INN YARD ON WASH-DAY!

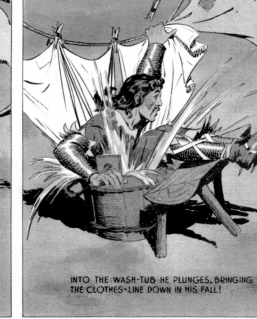

INTO THE WASH-TUB HE PLUNGES, BRINGING THE CLOTHES-LINE DOWN IN HIS FALL!

CALLING THE INNKEEPER'S WIFE, VAL POINTS TO THE TANGLED HEAP, "I FEAR SOME ONE IS STEALING YOUR WASH!"

"OH! YOU THIEF! (THUMP), YOU VARLET! (WHACK) YOU MISCREANT! (BANG) GET OUT OF MY WASHTUB!"

171 5-19-40   Copr. 1940, King Features Syndicate, Inc., World rights reserved.

BUT NOBLE SIR GAWAIN, MUCH AS HE WISHES, CANNOT GET OUT OF THE TUB. UNLESS HE RECEIVES HELP HE IS DOOMED TO WADDLE AROUND LIKE A TURTLE FOR THE REST OF HIS LIFE!

HAL FOSTER

NEXT WEEK — **Wounded Pride**

Prince Valiant

IN THE DAYS OF KING ARTHUR
BY HAROLD R FOSTER

Synopsis: WHEN SIR GAWAIN FINDS HE HAS BEEN CHEATED AT DICE BY THREE GAMBLERS HE FLIES INTO A RAGE AND WHIPS OUT HIS SWORD.....UNFORTUNATELY HE BECOMES ENTANGLED IN A CLOTHES-LINE AND A WASH-TUB. FOR SO NOBLE A KNIGHT HIS SITUATION IS MOST UNDIGNIFIED!

"VAL, TRISTRAM. HELP ME ELSE I FINISH MY STAY ON EARTH, AMBLING ABOUT LIKE A CONFOUNDED TURTLE!"

IT IS THE HALF-WITTED STABLE BOY WHO FINALLY SOLVES THE PROBLEM WITH THE SUGGESTION THAT THEY CUT THE HOOPS AND BRINGS FORWARD A SHARP HATCHET.

BUT THE BOY SADLY MISJUDGES THE FORCE NECESSARY TO CUT ONLY THE HOOP!

SOME INVALIDS GET SYMPATHY, BUT THE NATURE OF GAWAIN'S MISFORTUNE BRINGS FORTH ONLY JOKES AND LAUGHTER FROM HIS FRIENDS AND SCOWLS FROM HIM.

IT WILL BE TWO OR THREE DAYS BEFORE GAWAIN CAN RIDE AGAIN. HE GROANS AT THE ENFORCED IDLENESS.

MEANWHILE, TRISTRAM HAS TAKEN THE THREE GAMBLERS INTO THE INN YARD. *"IT IS THE CUSTOM OF ALL KNIGHTS TO DO SOME USEFUL DEED EACH DAY,"* HE EXPLAINS, *"NOW, I WILL SHARPEN THIS LONG SWORD OF MINE, AND YOU...?"* THEY EYE THE GLEAMING SWORD DUBIOUSLY AND SET TO WORK.

WHEN THEIR WORK IS FINISHED SIR TRISTRAM, WITH KNIGHTLY COURTESY, HELPS THEM ON THEIR WAY!

AS ALL TRUE KNIGHTS MUST PRACTISE CHIVALRY TO THE LADIES....TRISTRAM STROLLS TO THE SQUARE TO PRACTISE IT ON THE VILLAGE MAIDENS. THERE WERE NO COMPLAINTS.

HAL FOSTER

WHILE TO VAL, STROLLING IN THE OPPOSITE DIRECTION, COMES A BREATHLESS PEASANT......*"THE GIANT, THE GIANT COMES!"*

NEXT WEEK— **The Giant.**

Prince Valiant

Synopsis: WHILE TRISTRAM, PRINCE VALIANT AND SIR GAWAIN ARE JOURNEYING TOWARD ROME THEY ARE DELAYED IN A MOUNTAIN VILLAGE WHILE GAWAIN RECOVERS FROM AN ACCIDENT. SUDDENLY A SHOUT GOES UP. *"THE GIANT, THE GIANT!"*

LOOKING UP THE ROAD, VAL SEES NO FEARSOME GIANT, BUT ONLY A POMPOUS LITTLE DWARF, WADDLING TOWARD THEM ON HIS SHORT, BOWED LEGS.

HALTING, THE DWARF FROWNS IMPORTANTLY AND READS FROM A LIST THE ARTICLES DEMANDED BY THE GIANT, *"SEND THESE ON TWO WORK-HORSES LED BY A MALE SLAVE OR MY TERRIBLE MASTER WILL COME IN ANGER!"*

"TWICE EACH YEAR," EXPLAINS THE VILLAGE CHIEF, "THE GIANT MAKES DEMANDS ON ALL THE HAMLETS HEREABOUT..... MANY HAVE SOUGHT TO KILL HIM..... NONE HAVE RETURNED!"

"I WILL BE THAT SLAVE AND I WILL RETURN... I HOPE!" SAYS VAL, THROWING A CLOAK OVER THE GREAT *"SINGING SWORD".*

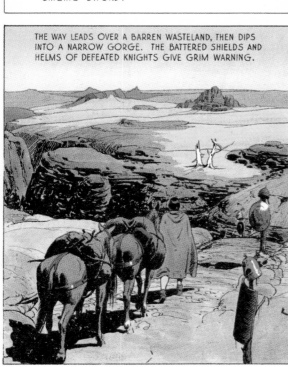

THE WAY LEADS OVER A BARREN WASTELAND, THEN DIPS INTO A NARROW GORGE. THE BATTERED SHIELDS AND HELMS OF DEFEATED KNIGHTS GIVE GRIM WARNING.

A WEIRD, SHADOWY PLACE OF FANTASTIC SHAPES AND BROODING SILENCE..... ALMOST ANYTHING IS MORE THAN LIKELY TO HAPPEN HERE..... VAL HAS THE STRANGE FEELING OF BEING WATCHED!

NEXT WEEK—
The Watcher.

Prince Valiant

IN THE DAYS OF KING ARTHUR
BY HAROLD R. FOSTER

Synopsis: FOR YEARS A TERRIBLE GIANT HAS DEMANDED TRIBUTE OF SLAVES AND SUPPLIES FROM THE SURROUNDING VILLAGES. HAVING SOME IDLE TIME ON HIS HANDS, PRINCE VALIANT THINKS IT MIGHT BE ENTERTAINING TO RID THE WORLD OF THIS MENACE.... HE GOES IN PLACE OF THE SLAVE.

AS HE LEADS THE LADEN HORSES DOWN THE FEARFUL CHASM, HE FEELS AS THOUGH STRANGE EYES ARE WATCHING HIM.

HE STEALS A QUICK GLANCE BEHIND AND SEES THAT WHICH HE FEARS MOST TO FIND. AGAINST A FANTASTIC BACKGROUND IS A FANTASTIC MONSTER, HUGE AND MENACING.

VAL WALKS ON, WONDERING. HE MUST HAVE PASSED RIGHT BY THE MONSTER, YET HIS HORSES HAD SHOWN NO FEAR. TIMID, WILD CREATURES GAMBOL ABOUT THE GIANT'S FEET THERE MUST BE SOME ANSWER.

THE CANYON NARROWS TO A MERE CRACK IN WHICH A STRONG GATE-WAY IS SET....... THERE IS NO TURNING BACK NOW.

PASSING THROUGH, VAL STEALS A BACKWARD GLANCE — THE GIANT IS LOCKING THE MASSIVE GATES....TRAPPED!

THE TRAIL DESCENDS INTO A GROVE OF TREES AND THERE VAL TAKES THE BOW AND ARROWS HE HAD CONCEALED AND DISAPPEARS AMONG THE FOLIAGE.

SOON THE HUGE CREATURE GOES STRIDING BY!

AT THE END OF THE WOODS HE DISCOVERS THE ABSENCE OF THE NEW SLAVE.....WHEELING ABOUT HE SHOUTS HOARSELY, *"YOU CANNOT ESCAPE. YOU MUST COME TO ME OR STARVE!"*

174 6-9-40

AS HE TURNS HOMEWARD, A YELPING PACK OF OUTCAST DOGS SURROUNDS HIM, LEAPING AND BARKING.

NEXT WEEK— **A Strange Household**

Prince Valiant

IN THE DAYS OF KING ARTHUR
BY HAROLD R FOSTER

Synopsis: PRINCE VALIANT UNDERTAKES A QUEST TO RID THE COUNTRY-SIDE OF A TROUBLESOME GIANT. FAR OUT IN A BARREN WASTELAND IS A GREEN VALLEY, ITS ONLY ENTRANCE GUARDED BY A STRONG GATEWAY....THE WILY GIANT CLOSES THIS GATEWAY BEHIND THE PRINCE. FROM A TREE-TOP VAL WATCHES THE MONSTER STRIDING HOMEWARD WITH HIS YELPING DOGS.

LIKE A GOOD GENERAL VAL DECIDES TO PLAN A RETREAT BEFORE VENTURING ON AN ATTACK. THE STREAM THAT WATERS THIS RICH VALLEY MUST HAVE AN OUTLET......

......BUT THE OUTLET FALLS SHEER INTO A STILL LOWER CANYON.

NOR CAN HE SCALE THE WALLS.... BELOW HIM GRAZE FLOCKS OF SHEEP AND FAT CATTLE. SLAVES WORK IN THE SUNNY FIELDS.

AT SUNDOWN HE REPAIRS AGAIN TO THE WOOD AND THERE BUSIES HIMSELF UNTIL DARK.

SILENTLY, THROUGH THE VELVETY DARKNESS, VAL CREEPS TO THE GIANT'S HOUSE AND RAISES HIS CROOK TO THE TOP OF THE WALL.

ONCE ON THE WALL HE CAN REACH THE LEDGE OF A LIGHTED WINDOW. FROM WITHIN COMES A CONFUSED MEDLEY OF STRANGE VOICES.

VAL PEERS THROUGH THE SHUTTERS ON A NIGHTMARE SCENE.... AROUND THAT LITTERED BOARD ARE GATHERED THE DEFORMED, THE MISSHAPEN, THE CRIPPLED, THE HALF-WITTED, DWARF AND GIANT....THE WORLD'S OUTCASTS.

NEXT WEEK—
Prince Valiant meets the Giant.

175 6-16-40

Prince Valiant

IN THE DAYS OF
KING ARTHUR
BY
HAROLD R FOSTER

Synopsis: PRINCE VALIANT HAS COME TO THIS HIDDEN VALLEY TO KILL A FEARSOME GIANT WHO HAS TERRORIZED THE COUNTRYSIDE FOR YEARS. VAL IS FRANKLY PUZZLED THAT SO DREAD A MONSTER SHOULD KEEP AND CARE FOR ALL THE OUTCASTS, WHETHER MAN OR BEAST.

AT LAST VAL THINKS HE HAS THE ANSWER TO THE PUZZLE . . . . IN THE MORNING HE WILL PUT IT TO THE TEST.

SO AT SUN-UP HE TAKES HIS STAND IN FULL VIEW . . . . HIS BOW AND QUIVER OF ARROWS CONCEALED BEHIND HIS CLOAK.

"SO," BELLOWS THE GIANT, "OUR NEW SLAVE HAS DECIDED TO WORK RATHER THAN STARVE."

SUDDENLY VAL WHIPS OUT HIS BOW. "MOVE BUT ONE MORE STEP," HE CRIES, "AND I'LL SHOOT EVERY DOG IN YOUR PACK!"

THE HEAVY, STUPID FACE OF THE GIANT LOSES ITS EVIL SCOWL; FOR A MOMENT HE SEEMS PUZZLED, THEN A LOOK OF SORROW COMES INTO HIS EYES. "NO, NO," HE CRIES, "DON'T HARM MY FRIENDS!"

"THEY ARE BUT POOR OUTCASTS FROM THE CRUELTY OF SUCH AS YOU. SPARE THEM AND YOU MAY GO FREE. I HAVE MADE THIS VALLEY A REFUGE FOR ALL WHO HAVE SUFFERED THE SNEERS AND ABUSE OF MEN . . . . GO, BUT KEEP OUR SECRET!"

HAL FOSTER

NEXT WEEK -
The Life of a Giant.

176 6-23-40

Prince Valiant

Synopsis: PRINCE VALIANT SETS OUT TO KILL A TERRIBLE GIANT; INSTEAD HE HUMBLES THAT GIANT BY THREATENING TO KILL HIS BELOVED DOGS. THE GIANT TELLS HIS STORY.

3. WHILE STILL A BOY I WAS SO HUGE THAT MY POOR PARENTS COULD NO LONGER FEED ME.

2. "AT FIRST I WAS LIKE ANY OTHER CHILD, BUT SOMETHING HAPPENED TO ME.... INSIDE. I STARTED TO GROW RAPIDLY.

4. I WAS LOOKED UPON AS SOMETHING QUEER, TO BE LAUGHED AT, ABUSED, THE BUTT OF ALL JOKES..... IT WAS CRUEL.

5. IN DESPERATION I LEFT MY VILLAGE, BUT STRANGERS LOOKED UPON ME WITH HORROR. IN THEIR FEAR THEY CALLED ME A MONSTER.

7. MANY KNIGHTS HAVE SOUGHT TO KILL ME, BUT I WIELD A MORE TERRIBLE WEAPON THAN ANY KNIGHT CAN CARRY.

HAL FOSTER

1.

6. I SOON LEARNED TO TAKE ADVANTAGE OF THEIR FEAR TO GET WHAT I NEEDED.

8. AT LAST I FOUND THIS VALLEY... SINCE THEN I HAVE MADE IT A HAVEN TO ALL WHO, LIKE ME, HAVE SUFFERED FROM MAN'S CRUELTY... THE MAIMED, THE TWISTED, THE DWARF, THE WITCH; ALL WHO ARE OUTCASTS."

NEXT WEEK:
The Giant's Victory

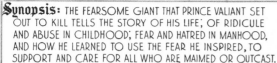

Synopsis: THE FEARSOME GIANT THAT PRINCE VALIANT SET OUT TO KILL TELLS THE STORY OF HIS LIFE; OF RIDICULE AND ABUSE IN CHILDHOOD; FEAR AND HATRED IN MANHOOD, AND HOW HE LEARNED TO USE THE FEAR HE INSPIRED, TO SUPPORT AND CARE FOR ALL WHO ARE MAIMED OR OUTCAST.

"AND NOW YOU HAVE LEARNED MY SECRET," SAYS THE GIANT SADLY. "PEOPLE WILL NO LONGER FEAR ME- MY FRIENDS WILL STARVE."

"I SYMPATHIZE WITH YOU. NEVER-THE-LESS, I'VE PLEDGED MY KNIGHT-LY WORD TO RID THE COUNTRYSIDE OF YOUR MENACE AND I WILL KEEP MY VOW.....BUT, IN THIS MANNER....."

......"LOOK, YOUR FIELDS ARE FERTILE; YOUR HERDS AND FLOCKS INCREASE; YOU HAVE WEALTH BEYOND YOUR NEEDS. SO OPEN YOUR GATES TO COMMERCE WITH YOUR NEIGHBORS. EXCHANGE THEIR FEAR FOR THEIR RESPECT!"

"TRUST! FRIENDLINESS! THINGS I'VE NEVER KNOWN....TO BE A RESPECTED LANDOWNER, TOO GOOD TO BE TRUE, BUT I'LL TRY IT!"

CALLING HIS SLAVES TOGETHER, THE GIANT ANNOUNCES, "I GIVE YOU ALL YOUR FREEDOM. ANY WHO WISHES TO REMAIN WILL BE PAID A FAIR WAGE, GOOD FOOD AND LODGINGS."

THE GATES ARE FLUNG WIDE AND ALL THE WORKERS RUSH OUT TO FREEDOM, SHOUTING JOYOUSLY!

"YOUR IDEA WAS TOO GOOD TO BE TRUE! LOOK, MY FIELDS AND FLOCKS ARE UNATTENDED. NOBODY WILL WILLINGLY WORK FOR ONE THEY FEAR!"

"A MAN NEVER VALUES WHAT HE HAS, ONLY THAT WHICH HE CANNOT HAVE. WHEN THEY HAVE ENJOYED THEIR NEW-FOUND LIBERTY THEY WILL REMEMBER YOUR FAIR TREAT-MENT. SEE! EVEN NOW, SOME ARE RETURNING......."

178 7-7-40

MOUNTED ON A WORK HORSE, VAL RETURNS TO HIS FRIENDS. "THE UNHAPPY SLAVES OF YESTERDAY WILL BE CONTENTED WORKERS TO-MORROW, AND ONLY BECAUSE A DISTANT GATE IS NOW UNLATCHED. WHO WAS IT THAT SAID, 'MONKEYS ARE THE CRAZIEST PEOPLE'"?

NEXT WEEK— **Target Practice.**

Prince Valiant

IN THE DAYS OF
KING ARTHUR
BY
HAROLD R FOSTER

Registered U. S. Patent Office

Synopsis: AND SO PRINCE VALIANT RIDES BACK FROM THE VALLEY OF THE GIANT. THE GIANT IS NO LONGER A MENACE, BUT PROMISES TO BECOME A RESPECTABLE LANDED SQUIRE.

"THE GIANT OFFERS GOOD WAGES FOR WORKERS ON HIS RICH ESTATE AND WILL TRADE IN CATTLE AND GRAIN WITH HIS NEIGHBORS. TREAT HIM WITH RESPECT AND YOU NEED NO LONGER FEAR HIM."

"THAT QUEST IS FINISHED. SO, MY COMRADES, IF GAWAIN'S DISTRESSING WOUND HAS HEALED WE CAN DEPART."

WITH MUCH GROANING SIR GAWAIN GETS PAINFULLY INTO HIS WELL-PADDED SADDLE AND THEY SET OUT ONCE MORE FOR ROME.

THEIR JOURNEY IS UNEVENTFUL UNTIL THE BLUE OF THE ADRIATIC SEA GLEAMS ON THE HORIZON. THEN THEY COME ACROSS A BAND OF TRAVELING MER-CHANTS, HIDING BEHIND A LOW HILL.

"WE FEAR TO PROCEED, FOR YONDER SENTRY GIVES WARNING THAT RAIDING HUNS MUST BE CAMPED BELOW."

IT IS DEEMED ADVISABLE TO REMOVE THE SENTRY QUIETLY WITH AN ARROW, BUT THIS GIVES RISE TO AN ARGUMENT AS TO WHO IS BEST QUALIFIED FOR THE SHOT!

SO WAGERS ARE LAID, ARROWS CHOSEN WITH CARE AND, AT A GIVEN SIGNAL, THREE BOWS TWANG.

IT WAS RATHER TOUGH ON THE SENTRY BUT, AS TRISTRAM SAID AFTERWARD, HE WOULD HAVE DONE AS MUCH FOR US, IF HE HAD SEEN US FIRST.

IT IS JUST AS THE MERCHANTS SUSPECTED. BELOW THE SENTRY'S POST A BAND OF RAIDING HUNS IS ENCAMPED!

NEXT WEEK— **The Stampede.**

179 7-14-40

HAL FOSTER

Prince Valiant

Synopsis: THE ROAD TO ROME WINDS DOWN FROM THE HILLS TO THE MARSHY PLAINS BORDERING THE ADRIATIC SEA AND THERE, BLOCKING THE PATH, IS AN ENCAMPMENT OF HUN RAIDERS.

THE BARBARIANS LOLL BY THE CAMPFIRES, WHILE THEIR HORSES GRAZE. AND ON A FAR RIDGE, SCOUTS ARE SPYING ON THEIR INTENDED VICTIMS, A GROUP OF WORKERS NEAR THE SEA.

ONE OF THE MERCHANTS IS DRESSED IN THE LATE SENTRY'S GARMENTS AND STANDS ON GUARD SO THE RAIDERS BELOW WILL NOT BECOME SUSPICIOUS.

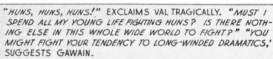

"HUNS, HUNS, HUNS!" EXCLAIMS VAL TRAGICALLY. "MUST I SPEND ALL MY YOUNG LIFE FIGHTING HUNS? IS THERE NOTHING ELSE IN THIS WHOLE WIDE WORLD TO FIGHT?" "YOU MIGHT FIGHT YOUR TENDENCY TO LONG-WINDED DRAMATICS," SUGGESTS GAWAIN.

"NOW, VAL, HOW ABOUT A QUAINT AND AMUSING SCHEME TO LEND THE SPICE OF NOVELTY TO OUR COMING FUSS WITH THE ENEMY?"

"I HAVE IT! THE HUNS ARE RENOWNED HORSEMEN IT WOULD DISCOURAGE THEM GREATLY TO BE TRAMPLED TO DEATH BY THEIR OWN HORSES!"

SEVERAL OF THE MORE VENTURESOME OF THE MERCHANTS ARE GIVEN GREAT TORCHES AND MOUNTED ON PACK ANIMALS. BY A ROUND-ABOUT WAY THEY APPROACH THE RAIDERS' GRAZING MOUNTS.

WITH FLAMING TORCHES, WAVING CLOAKS AND SCREAMING LIKE DEMONS THEY CHARGE DOWN UPON THE STARTLED HERD.....AND THE STAMPEDE IS ON!

NEXT WEEK— **Venice is Born.**

Prince Valiant

Synopsis: THE ROAD TO ROME LEADS DOWN FROM THE SNOWY ALPS TO THE VENETIAN PLAINS AND THERE THE WAY IS BLOCKED BY THE CAMP OF A BAND OF HUNS. CLOSE TO THEM IN THE NARROW VALLEY GRAZE THE RAIDERS' HORSES. PRINCE VALIANT, TRISTRAM AND SIR GAWAIN MAKE QUICK PLANS TO WIN THROUGH.

HOWLING LIKE DEMONS AND WITH BLAZING TORCHES AND WAVING CLOAKS, THEY SWOOP DOWN UPON THE STARTLED MOUNTS... THE STAMPÉDE IS ON! AND THE HUNS, MOST RENOWNED OF HORSEMEN, SUFFER THE IGNOMINY OF BEING TRAMPLED INTO THE DUST BY THEIR OWN STEEDS!

OUT ACROSS THE PLAIN THEY DRIVE THE HORSES WITHOUT BOTHERING ABOUT THEIR BATTERED OWNERS, FOR THE HUN IS HELPLESS WHEN SET AFOOT.

SEVERAL MILES FARTHER ON THE THREE COMRADES MEET THE HUNS' INTENDED VICTIMS. *"WE ARE THE VENETI, HUNGARY IS ON OUR EASTERN BORDER AND THE HUNS HAVE DRIVEN US FROM OUR HOMELAND TO SEEK SAFETY ON ISLANDS FAR OUT ON THE ADRIATIC SEA."*

"WE MUST HAVE STONE FOR BUILDING AND TIMBER FOR SHIPS, BUT THE HUNS HARRY OUR WORKMEN. WE CANNOT PREVAIL AGAINST THE BARBARIANS."

WHEN THE VENETI LEARN THAT THESE THREE KNIGHTS ARE THE FAMOUS LEADERS OF THE "HUN-HUNTERS" THEY PLEAD WITH THEM TO ORGANIZE AN ARMY OF DEFENSE.

WHILE SIR GAWAIN TURNS VENTURESOME YOUNG MEN INTO SWIFT, HARD-RIDING CAVALRY, PRINCE VALIANT TRAINS STEADY FOOT SOLDIERS IN THE METHODS HE FOUND SO SUCCESSFUL IN HIS RECENT CAMPAIGN AGAINST THEIR ENEMY.....

.....TRISTRAM PICKS THE BEST OF THE VENETI MANHOOD AND PATIENTLY, TIRELESSLY TRAINS THEM TO OFFICER THE TROOP.

THEN THEY GO HAPPILY ON THEIR WAY, RICHER NOW, BUT QUITE UNAWARE THAT THEY HAVE HELPED IN THE BUILDING OF VENICE....VENICE, THE BEAUTIFUL, SOON TO RIVAL IN GRANDEUR AND POWER EVEN ROME, ITSELF!

NEXT WEEK— **Duck-Hunting.**

181 7-28-40

Prince Valiant

IN THE DAYS OF
KING ARTHUR
BY
HAROLD R. FOSTER

Synopsis: AS THE THREE KNIGHTS OF THE ROUND TABLE, TRISTRAM, PRINCE VALIANT AND SIR GAWAIN, JOURNEY ALONG THE SHORES OF THE ADRIATIC SEA, THEY MEET WITH THE VENETI TRIBES AND HELP THEM ESTABLISH A CITY, FAR OUT IN THE SEA, AWAY FROM THE MENACE OF PLUNDERING HUNS. LITTLE DID THEY KNOW, OR CARE, THAT THEY WERE HELPING FOUND THE CITY OF VENICE!

AT LAST THEY REACH PADOVA, THEIR FIRST GREAT ROMAN CITY; THE SQUALID POVERTY OF THE PRESENT LIVING AMID THE RUINED SPLENDOR OF THE PAST.

HERE THEY BUY SUPPLIES AND A RICH PAVILION; HIRE ATTENDANTS AND PROCEED ONWARD IN A STYLE MORE BEFITTING THEIR RANK. THE HEAVY TREAD OF INVADING ARMIES HAD LONG SINCE BROUGHT RUIN TO THE FAMED ROMAN ROADS.

FAR OUT ON THE WIDE MARSHES OF THE PO THEY BEHOLD A STRANGE SIGHT.....WAVE AFTER WAVE OF WILDFOWL COME, WINGING OVER THE DISTANT ALPS TO CIRCLE AND GLIDE DOWN AMONG THE TALL REEDS.

TEAL AND WIDGEON, BRANT AND GEESE, SNIPE AND GOLDEN PLOVER....ALL THE FAMILIAR WATERFOWL OF DISTANT ENGLAND....BRINGING RUMOR OF WINTRY STORMS IN THEIR MISTY NORTHERN HOMELAND.
THE PAVILION IS PITCHED AND THE THREE FRIENDS ABANDON THEMSELVES TO THE SPORT THEY USED TO ENJOY IN THE ENGLISH FENS.

LONG, HARD MONTHS OF FIGHTING LAY BEHIND THEM; ROME AND UNKNOWN ADVENTURES LIE AHEAD.... IN THE MEANTIME, THEY RELAX AND LET THE SUNNY, CAREFREE DAYS SLIP BY.

AT LAST THEY MOVE ON AGAIN, FOLLOWING THE RUINED ROAD UNTIL, IN THE DISTANCE, THEY BEHOLD THE WHITE TOWERS OF RAVENNA SHIMMERING IN THE SUNLIGHT....

....IN THE SHADOW OF THE CITY'S GATE A SOMBER FIGURE IN ORIENTAL GARB AWAITS THEIR COMING.

NEXT WEEK— **The Oriental.**

Synopsis: AFTER A WEEK OF HUNTING, THE THREE KNIGHTS OF THE ROUND TABLE RESUME THEIR LEISURELY JOURNEY TOWARD ROME. EVERYWHERE THEY ENCOUNTER RUIN AND DECAY. THE EMPIRE IS CRUMBLING. IN FACT, HERE AT RAVENNA, JUST TWENTY YEARS LATER, A WHITE-FACED BOY-EMPEROR WILL GIVE THE EMPIRE OVER TO THE BARBARIANS.

AS THEY ENTER THE CITY'S GATES, A STOOPED FIGURE IN ORIENTAL GARB APPRAISES THEM WITH KEEN EYES.

RAVENNA, THE BEAUTIFUL, GLEAMING WHITE IN THE SUNLIGHT! NEVER HAVE THESE NORTHERN KNIGHTS SEEN SUCH BUILDINGS, EVEN CAMELOT, THAT CITY OF MARVELS, CANNOT MATCH THE SPLENDOR OF ITS CARVED MARBLE AND SINGING FOUNTAINS!

FOR A WEEK THEY LINGER AMONG THE MANY WONDERS. THE WEALTH OF ITS LIBRARIES FASCINATES VAL.

AT NIGHT THEY REVEL IN THE LUXURY OF ROMAN ENTERTAINMENT

LIGHT-HEARTEDLY SIR GAWAIN SETS OUT TO LEARN THE LOCAL CUSTOMS AND DOES RIGHT WELL, DESPITE HIS LIMITED KNOWLEDGE OF LATIN.

TRISTRAM FINDS LIGHT EXERCISE IN A DUEL OR TWO. IT IS ALL GOOD CLEAN FUN AND NO ONE IS INJURED TOO SERIOUSLY.

AS THEY PREPARE TO LEAVE, THE ORIENTAL APPEARS.— "NOBLE SIRS, YE BE KNIGHTS OF TABLE ROUND, BOUND BY OATH TO PUNISH WRONG AND BRING JUSTICE TO THE WEAK... I AM A JEWEL MERCHANT ROBBED OF HALF MY WEALTH BY THE GUARDS I HIRED TO PROTECT ME. EVEN NOW THEY LIE IN WAIT FOR ME ALONG THE ROAD, PLANNING FURTHER ROBBERY. MAY I BEG YOUR PROTECTION UNTIL THAT DANGER IS PAST?"

NEXT WEEK—
Let the Punishment Fit the Crime!

Copr. 1940, King Features Syndicate, Inc. World rights reserved.

HAL FOSTER

Prince Valiant

Synopsis: AS TRISTRAM, PRINCE VALIANT AND SIR GAWAIN ARE PREPARING TO LEAVE THE CITY OF RAVENNA, AN ORIENTAL JEWEL MERCHANT TELLS OF BEING ROBBED BY THE GUARDS HE HAD HIRED TO DEFEND HIM AND ASKS THEIR PROTECTION ON THE ROAD TO ROME.

"EVEN NOW, MY UNFAITHFUL SERVANTS WAIT IN THE WILDERNESS BEYOND TO ROB ME OF THE REST OF MY GOODS."

"OUR SWORDS ARE EVER PLEDGED TO DEFEND THE WEAK FROM OPPRESSION," SAYS TRISTRAM, "AND WE WILL AS QUICKLY DIVORCE YOUR HEAD FROM YOUR BODY IF YOU ARE DECEIVING US." SO THEY LET THE MERCHANT TRAVEL WITH THEM.

"LOOK!" CRIES THE MERCHANT, "YONDER BUSHES SHAKE; SOMEONE IS HIDING THERE AND HONEST MEN DON'T HIDE."

STRIDING INTO THE THICKET. VAL FINDS A CAMPING PLACE, BUT ITS OCCUPANTS ARE FLEEING INTO THE SWAMP BEYOND.

VAL TAKES TWO LEATHERN BUCKLERS FROM THE SQUIRES AND BINDS THEM TO HIS FEET.......

...AND GOES GLIDING OVER THE QUAKING MARSH IN QUICK PURSUIT OF THE FLOUNDERING THIEVES.

SIR GAWAIN WATCHES VAL ROUND UP THE FUGITIVES AND HERD THEM BACK, "THE YOUNG PRINCE IS A LIGHTHEARTED SCATTER-BRAIN," HE SAYS "UNTIL A CRISIS COMES; THEN SO MANY TRICKS, SCHEMES AND IDEAS FILL HIS HEAD IT HUMS LIKE A BEE-HIVE!"

WITH ALL HIS GLITTERING MERCHANDISE RESTORED TO HIM, THE ORIENTAL RAISES HIS ARMS IN SILENT THANKS TO THE STRANGE GODS OF HIS DISTANT HOME.

THE PUNISHMENT OF THE THIEVES IS LEFT TO THE MOSQUITOES, AS THEY ARE CHASED, NAKED, BACK INTO THE SWAMP.

NEXT WEEK— **Crossing the Rubicon.**

184 8-18-40

Synopsis: AN ORIENTAL JEWEL MERCHANT, WHO HAS BEEN ROBBED BY HIS ESCORT, PLACES HIMSELF UNDER THE PROTECTION OF THE THREE KNIGHTS. HIS UNFAITHFUL SERVANTS LIE IN WAIT FOR FURTHER PLUNDER, BUT ARE CAUGHT AND THE GEMS RESTORED TO THE OVERJOYED MERCHANT.

"IT IS THE LAW OF THE LAND THAT THIEVES MUST LOSE THEIR RIGHT HAND, BUT IT IS TOO PLEASANT A DAY TO SPOIL WITH BLOODSHED," SAYS TRISTRAM, "WE WILL LET THE MOSQUITOES OF YONDER SWAMP PUNISH YOU. UNDRESS!"

IT IS, INDEED, A GLORIOUS DAY, AND THEIR SONGS AND LAUGHTER MATCH THE BRIGHTNESS OF THE SUNLIT HOURS.

AT A RUINED BRIDGE VAL DISMOUNTS AND READS A WEATHERED INSCRIPTION — "THE RIVER RUBICON."

WITH MOCK GRAVITY VAL EXCLAIMS:- "HERE, WHERE I STAND, LONG AGO STOOD CAESAR. CAESAR MADE HIS DECISION, CROSSED THE RUBICON AND TOOK ROME. WHEN ROMAN ENVOYS DEMANDED TRIBUTE OF KING ARTHUR, HE UNCEREMONIOUSLY HUSTLED THEM OUT OF ENGLAND. AS ENGLISH KNIGHTS, WE MAY NOT BE SO POPULAR IN ROME!"

"LET'S CROSS, ANYWAY," SAYS GAWAIN. "EVEN IF WE DON'T TAKE ROME, ITSELF, WE MAY CAPTURE A TENDER HEART, A ROGUISH SMILE...." "YOU ARE A DESIGNING KNAVE," INTERRUPTS TRISTRAM, "AND NO FIT COMPANY FOR VAL AND ME."

BUT THE MERCHANT HESITATES TO FOLLOW, FOR FEAR HIS RICH GARMENTS WILL SUFFER.

INSTEAD HE CHOOSES THE CARELESSLY REPAIRED BRIDGE AND URGES HIS MOUNT TO CROSS.

THE ROTTED TIMBERS CREAK, SWAY CRAZILY AND COME CRASHING DOWN INTO THE MUDDY WATERS!

NEXT WEEK— **The Magic Charm.**

185 8-25-40

Prince Valiant

IN THE DAYS OF KING ARTHUR
BY HAROLD R FOSTER

Synopsis: WHEN LEAVING RAVENNA AN ORIENTAL JEWEL MERCHANT BEGS THEIR PROTECTION ON THE JOURNEY TO ROME, FOR HE HAS BEEN ROBBED ONCE AND FEARS ANOTHER ATTACK FROM THE SAME THIEVES. VAL CAPTURES THE ROBBERS AND RESTORES THE MISSING GEMS.

AT THE CROSSING OF THE RUBICON THE MERCHANT TRIES THE RUINED BRIDGE AND FALLS.

TRAPPED AMID THE WRECKAGE, THE STRUGGLING MAN SINKS BELOW THE MURKY WATER. VAL PLUNGES TO THE RESCUE.

THE CURRENT HAS GOUGED A DEEP POOL BENEATH THE BRIDGE AND VAL, FEELING ABOUT ITS DEPTHS WITH HIS LANCE, FINDS THE UNFORTUNATE MERCHANT.

CAUGHT IN THE SWIRLING WRECKAGE, VAL IS SWEPT IN AND, WEIGHED DOWN BY HIS ARMOR, BARELY GAINS THE SHALLOWS.

BUT HE DOES AND DRAGS HIS PRIZE ASHORE, TOO !

FIRST AID. ACCORDING TO AN OLD MANUSCRIPT: — "THOUGH WATER MAY SEEM TO HAVE QUENCHED THE FLAME OF LIFE THAT WARMS THE HEART A SPARK MAY YET REMAIN. BY USING THE LUNGS AS A BELLOWS THE SMOLDERING EMBER MAY BE FANNED ONCE MORE IN-TO LIVING FLAME."

AND LONG AND LONG THE REVIVED MERCHANT FUMBLES IN HIS LEATHERN POUCH. AT LAST HE HOLDS OUT THREE GLORIOUS GEMS. *"ONE FOR EACH OF YOU,"* HE SAYS, AND HIS FACE IS WHITE WITH ANGUISH AS HE PARTS WITH HIS BELOVED JEWELS.

"AND TO YOU, WHO WOULD UNHESITATINGLY RISK HIS LIFE FOR A STRANGER AND FOREIGNER, I GIVE THIS POTENT CHARM. HE WHO WEARS IT CAN NEVER BE BOUND BY CHAINS."

"MY STRONG RIGHT ARM AND THE 'SINGING SWORD' ARE A MUCH BETTER GUARANTEE AGAINST CHAINS!" LAUGHS VAL. BUT THEN, VAL CANNOT LOOK INTO THE FUTURE.

NEXT WEEK— **Roman General.**

186 9-1-40

Prince Valiant

Synopsis: THE MYSTERIOUS ORIENTAL SELLER OF JEWELS HAS GIVEN PRINCE VALIANT A NECKLACE, AS A REWARD FOR SAVING HIS LIFE...A CHARMED NECKLACE, FOR HE WHO WEARS IT, CAN NEVER BE BOUND BY CHAINS.

"A VERY PLAIN ORNAMENT TO BE TREASURED BY A DEALER IN PRECIOUS GEMS," VAL REMARKS, "LOOKS LIKE VERY HARD IRON DISKS WITH ROUGH EDGES. I WILL STILL PUT MY RELIANCE IN THE 'SINGING SWORD'."

IN ARIMINUM, THE CITY WHERE ROADS MEET, THE ORIENTAL MURMURS HIS GRATITUDE AND FAREWELL AND SILENTLY DISAPPEARS.

HARDLY ARE THEY SEATED IN A TAVERN WHEN A GREAT SHOUTING IS HEARD FROM THE STREETS: "AETIUS AND HIS LEGIONS APPROACH!"

SOON THE TRAMP OF MARCHING MEN IS HEARD AND AETIUS LEADS THE WEARY REMNANT OF HIS LEGIONS INTO THE CITY.

AETIUS, LAST OF THE GREAT ROMAN GENERALS, HERO OF THE BATTLE OF CHALONS, WHERE THE MAD CAREER OF ATTILA, THE HUN, WAS HALTED. HIS TIRED FACE IS LINED WITH SORROW, FOR HE KNOWS THE EMPIRE IS CRUMBLING, DESPITE HIS HEROIC TRIUMPHS. HE RETURNS NOW TO ROME AND AN UNDESERVED DOOM.

THAT EVENING THREE OF ENGLAND'S FINEST PAY A VISIT TO ROME'S GREATEST. WARRIORS ALL, THEY SOON BECOME FRIENDS.

ONCE AGAIN ON THE ROAD TO ROME, THIS TIME DOWN THE FAMED FLAMINIAN WAY AND FOR THE FIRST TIME IN MANY WEARY MONTHS THE FAITHFUL SOLDIERS HEAR THEIR GENERAL LAUGH.

ROME AT LAST, HER CARVED MARBLE ALL ROSY IN THE RAYS OF THE SETTING SUN, SPREAD LIKE A GLEAMING MANTLE OVER HER SEVEN HILLS.

NEXT WEEK— **The Emperor**

187 9-8-40 Copr. 1940, King Features Syndicate, Inc., World rights reserved.

Prince Valiant

IN THE DAYS OF
KING ARTHUR
BY
HAROLD R FOSTER

Synopsis: DOWN THE FLAMINIAN WAY MARCH THE WEARY SURVIVORS OF ROME'S VICTORIOUS ARMIES LED BY AETIUS, LAST OF THE GREAT ROMAN GENERALS. AETIUS IS IN GAY COMPANY, FOR BESIDE HIM RIDE TRISTRAM, PRINCE VALIANT AND SIR GAWAIN, HIS NEW-FOUND FRIENDS.

AT THE TIBER BRIDGE THEY PART, FOR AFTIUS IS TO MAKE A TRIUMPHAL ENTRY INTO ROME

IT IS NOT OFTEN NOW THAT THE CITIZENS CAN HAIL A VICTORIOUS GENERAL AND THEY GIVE THEIR HERO A WARM RECEPTION.

IN HIS PALACE THE EMPEROR VALENTINIAN IS SICK WITH FEAR AND ENVY. THE PEOPLE HATE HIM, HE HAS NO FRIENDS AND THE NOISY WELCOME OF HIS GREAT GENERAL FILLS HIS MEAN, VINDICTIVE HEART WITH A MURDEROUS JEALOUSY.

THE THREE COMRADES SOON FIND LUXURIOUS QUARTERS WITHIN THE CITY. VAL LOSES NO TIME IN SATISFYING HIS YOUTHFUL VANITY AND SOON APPEARS BATHED, PERFUMED AND ARRAYED IN THE LATEST ROMAN FASHION.

TRISTRAM FINDS HIS PLEASURE WITH THE YOUNG NOBLES OF THE PALACE GUARD, STUDIES THEIR MILITARY TACTICS AND JOINS IN THEIR ROUGH, WARLIKE GAMES.

ANYONE COULD PREDICT WHAT WOULD HAPPEN TO THE AMOROUS SIR GAWAIN.....HE FOLLOWED THE FIRST PAIR OF ROGUISH LATIN EYES THAT SMILE AT HIM, TO MAKE LIGHT-HEARTED LOVE..... AND TROUBLE!

IN A SECLUDED GARDEN WHERE FLOWERS BLOOM AND SILVERY FOUNTAINS PLAY, THE EMPEROR PLANS A SORDID DEED AND SEALS THE FATE OF ROME

NEXT WEEK- **Gawain and the Lady**

188 9-15-40

HAL FOSTER

Prince Valiant

Synopsis: AETIUS, THE GREAT GENERAL, HAS RETURNED TO ROME IN TRIUMPH. FOR YEARS HE HAS HELD BACK THE FIERCE BARBARIANS, BUT HIS POPULARITY HAS AROUSED THE VINDICTIVE JEALOUSY OF HIS EMPEROR.

WEAK VALENTINIAN PLOTS THE ASSASSINATION OF THE ONLY MAN WHO CAN SAVE THE TOTTERING EMPIRE FROM ITS WAITING ENEMIES.

MEANWHILE, SIR GAWAIN GAILY FOLLOWS THE LITTER OF THE LADY WHOSE DARK EYES HAD SMILED AT HIM.

OUTSIDE HER HOME HE WAITS FOR WOMAN'S WELL-KNOWN CURIOSITY TO REVEAL HER WINDOW, AND SURE ENOUGH, A SHUTTER OPENS SOFTLY AND A DARK EYE APPEARS IN THE CRACK.

AT MOONRISE HE RETURNS WITH VAL'S CRIMSON BORDERED CLOAK OVER HIS SHOULDERS AND GLIB NONSENSE ON HIS TONGUE. HE QUITE FORGETS TO ASK IF SHE IS MARRIED.....

AND SHE IS SO STARTLED TO FIND THIS HANDSOME FOREIGNER ON HER BALCONY THAT SHE FORGETS TO MENTION IT,.....FOR HOURS. HER HUSBAND, WHEN HE COMES HOME, IS STARTLED, TOO!

HE DOESN'T BELIEVE IN ROMANCE, HE IS JEALOUS... "FIND OUT WHO WEARS THAT CRIMSON-BORDERED CLOAK," HE ORDERS.

BUT WHEN NEXT THAT CLOAK APPEARS VAL IS WEARING IT AND NOT GAWAIN.

"SO-O-O, IT IS THIS YOUNG STRANGER, SIR VALIANT, WHO CLIMBS MY WALLS LIKE A MONKEY! ARM YOURSELVES, MEN, WE GO TO ENJOY A KILLING!"

AND AT THE SAME MOMENT VALENTINIAN'S DEADLY ASSASSINS SET FORTH TO MURDER AETIUS.

NEXT WEEK—
The Scene is Set.

189 9-22-40

Prince Valiant

AETIUS WANDERS IN THE DUSK ALONE. ALL HIS VICTORIES, HIS TRIUMPHS ARE HOLLOW, FOR THE WEAK AND COWARDLY EMPEROR UNDOES ALL HIS GOOD WORK.

THE EMPEROR VALENTINIAN, IN A JEALOUS RAGE, SENDS HIS ASSASSINS OUT AFTER AETIUS, CARING NOTHING FOR THE FATE OF HIS EMPIRE.

AND A JEALOUS HUSBAND GOES OUT TO FIND A TOO-ROMANTIC CAVALIER IN A SCARLET-BORDERED CLOAK.

SIR GAWAIN SINGS HAPPILY AS HE GOES TO SERENADE THE DARK-EYED MAID IN THE BIG HOUSE. HE HAS NOT BORROWED VAL'S CLOAK TONIGHT, BUT WEARS HIS OWN.

TRISTRAM AND PRINCE VALIANT, TIRED BUT HAPPY AFTER A DAY OF SIGHT-SEEING, STRIDE HOMEWARD TOWARD THEIR LODGINGS.

GAWAIN CLIMBS TO THE BALCONY OF THE BEWITCHING LITTLE FLIRT WHO, SOMEHOW, HAS NOT YET FOUND TIME TO TELL HIM SHE IS MARRIED.

IN A LOW VOICE TREMBLING WITH EMOTION, SIR GAWAIN SINGS AN OLD TAVERN SONG. SHE DOES NOT UNDERSTAND ENGLISH SO HE TELLS HER IT IS A TENDER LOVE BALLAD AND EVERYONE IS HAPPY.......

.... THAT IS, EVERYONE WAS HAPPY UNTIL THE HUSBAND SEES THE HATED SCARLET-BORDERED CLOAK!

THINKING THEY ARE BESET BY THIEVES, VAL AND TRISTRAM SWING LUSTILY AND NOW EVERYONE IS NICKED AND BRUISED, THAT IS, ALL EXCEPT GAWAIN, THE CAUSE OF IT ALL, WHO LOLLS COMFORTABLY ON A BALCONY!

NEXT WEEK—
The Deed.

190 9-29-40

Prince Valiant

Synopsis: TRISTRAM, PRINCE VALIANT AND SIR GAWAIN ARRIVE IN ROME JUST AT THE TIME WHEN INTRIGUE, JEALOUSY AND TREACHERY ARE BRINGING RUIN TO THE EMPIRE. THE EMPEROR, JEALOUS OF AETIUS' POPULARITY, HAS ORDERED HIS ASSASSINATION.

SIR GAWAIN GAYLY CROONS THE HOURS AWAY IN VERY CHARMING, BUT DANGEROUS, COMPANY. HE DOES NOT KNOW THAT, FOR HER SAKE, A FEW MILES AWAY........

.......HER JEALOUS HUSBAND, SHOWING LITTLE SKILL, BUT A GREAT DEAL OF BAD TEMPER, IS EXCHANGING NICKS AND BRUISES WITH THE INNOCENT VAL.

AND AETIUS, ATTRACTED BY THE CLAMOR, DOES NOT HEAR, UNTIL TOO LATE, THE APPROACH OF HIS EMPEROR'S BULLIES

SO THE LAST OF THE GREAT ROMAN GENERALS FALLS AT THE HANDS OF HIS EMPEROR'S BUSY ASSASSINS AND WITH HIM GOES THE LAST HOPE OF THE ROMAN EMPIRE.

BUT THE OFFICER IN COMMAND IS A BRIGHT YOUNG MAN. *"ARREST THOSE TWO ARMED FOREIGNERS FOR THE MURDER OF AETIUS, OUR BELOVED GENERAL!"*

NEXT WEEK— **Prison.**

Synopsis: A LIMP FIGURE LIES SPRAWLED IN THE STREET.... AETIUS, VICTOR OF MANY A FIERCE BATTLE, COULD NOT SURVIVE THE JEALOUS ENVY OF HIS EMPEROR. AND ROME, THE LAST OF HER GREAT GENERALS FOULLY MURDERED, BECOMES EASY PREY TO HER ENEMIES. TWENTY YEARS LATER THE EMPIRE FALLS TO THE BARBARIANS.

SIR TRISTRAM AND PRINCE VALIANT ARE WITNESSES TO THE SORDID DEED.....

....AND ARE PROMPTLY ARRESTED BY THE EMPEROR'S PRIVATE ASSASSINS AND ACCUSED OF THE MURDER.

ON THE WAY TO THE PRISON-FORTRESS THEY ARE GIVEN AMPLE OPPORTUNITY TO ESCAPE, BUT THEY KNOW THAT TRICK AND PREFER TO PROCLAIM THEIR INNOCENCE AT A TRIAL.

THEY ARE GIVEN QUARTERS BEFITTING THEIR RANK AND SUFFICIENT GUARDS TO INDICATE THEIR IMPORTANCE.

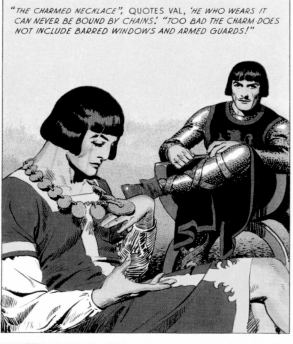

"THE CHARMED NECKLACE", QUOTES VAL, *'HE WHO WEARS IT CAN NEVER BE BOUND BY CHAINS.' "TOO BAD THE CHARM DOES NOT INCLUDE BARRED WINDOWS AND ARMED GUARDS!"*

NEXT DAY THEY HEAR A GREAT COMMOTION IN THE HALL AND THEIR GIDDY COMPANION, SIR GAWAIN, IS HUSTLED INTO THEIR PRISON. *"GOOD POLICE WORK"*, GREETS TRISTRAM. *"THE DAUGHTERS OF ROME CAN NOW WALK THEIR OWN STREETS WITHOUT BEING CHASED BY AN AMOROUS MORON!"*

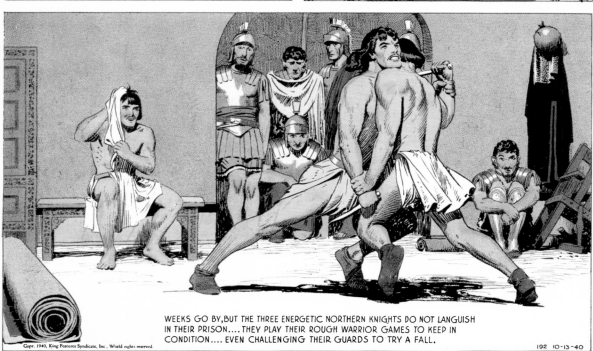

WEEKS GO BY, BUT THE THREE ENERGETIC NORTHERN KNIGHTS DO NOT LANGUISH IN THEIR PRISON.... THEY PLAY THEIR ROUGH WARRIOR GAMES TO KEEP IN CONDITION.... EVEN CHALLENGING THEIR GUARDS TO TRY A FALL.

192 10-13-40

AT LONG LAST THEY ARE SUMMONED TO TRIAL BEFORE THE EMPEROR, HIMSELF!

NEXT WEEK—
Valentinian's Justice

HAL FOSTER

Prince Valiant

Synopsis: EMPEROR VALENTINIAN IS WELL PLEASED WITH HIMSELF. IN A JEALOUS RAGE HE HAS HAD HIS GREAT GENERAL, AETIUS, FOULLY MURDERED AND THEN PUTS THE BLAME ON THE THREE ENGLISH VISITORS, TRISTRAM, PRINCE VALIANT AND SIR GAWAIN.

AFTER WEARY WEEKS OF WAITING, THEY ARE AT LAST SUMMONED TO TRIAL BEFORE THE EMPEROR.

"I DO NOT TRUST THIS EMPEROR'S JUSTICE," WHISPERS VAL, "BUT THE TIME FOR ESCAPE IS NOT YET. WHEN IT COMES, BE READY."

LIKE A BLOATED, POISONOUS TOAD THE EMPEROR SITS GLOATING AT HIS VICTIMS WITH PALE, VINDICTIVE EYES.

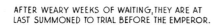

VALENTINIAN SPEAKS TO HIS FAWNING COURTIERS, "OUR VASSALS IN ENGLAND HAVE REBELLED AND REFUSE TO PAY TRIBUTE TO YOUR KIND EMPEROR. THEY HAVE EVEN SENT ASSASSINS TO MURDER OUR MOST ABLE AND BELOVED GENERAL. AS A WARNING WE WILL HAVE A PUBLIC EXECUTION WITH, SAY, FIRE. IT WILL ENTERTAIN OUR RESTLESS POPULACE."

THE FRIENDS OF AETIUS ARE MANY AND POWERFUL AND THEY CHOOSE THIS PARTICULAR TIME TO RIGHT A GREAT MANY WRONGS WITH ANOTHER WRONG.

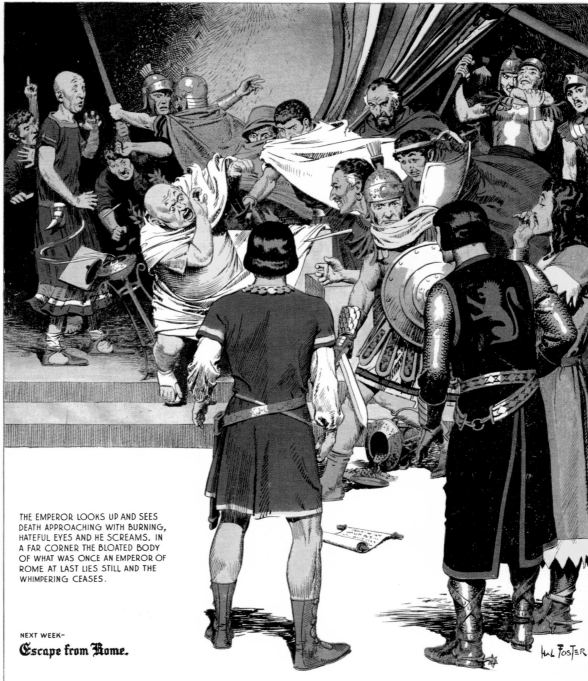

THE EMPEROR LOOKS UP AND SEES DEATH APPROACHING WITH BURNING, HATEFUL EYES AND HE SCREAMS. IN A FAR CORNER THE BLOATED BODY OF WHAT WAS ONCE AN EMPEROR OF ROME AT LAST LIES STILL AND THE WHIMPERING CEASES.

NEXT WEEK—
Escape from Rome.

HAL FOSTER

Prince Valiant

IN THE DAYS OF KING ARTHUR
BY
HAROLD R FOSTER

Synopsis: EMPEROR VALENTINIAN WAS CLEVER. IN A JEALOUS RAGE HE HAS AETIUS ASSASSINATED AND THE CRIME BLAMED ON THE THREE KNIGHTS OF THE ROUND TABLE. AT THEIR TRIAL FRIENDS OF AETIUS PUT AN END TO THEIR EMPEROR'S MISDEEDS WITH BECOMING GUSTO.

"THIS, TOO, WILL BE BLAMED ON US," WHISPERS VAL, "LET US ACT LIKE THE EMPEROR'S BRAVE COURTIERS!" AND THEY ALSO RUN LIKE FRIGHTENED RABBITS FROM THE HALL.

TO THEIR LODGINGS THEY RACE:

QUICKLY THEY ARM WHILE THE SQUIRES PACK THE SADDLE-BAGS.

THEY HAD MOVED SO SPEEDILY THAT THEY RIDE IN A LEISURELY, INNOCENT MANNER THROUGH THE EASTERN GATE BEFORE THE NEWS OF THE EMPEROR'S DEATH ARRIVES

"YOU WERE RIGHT, VAL," OBSERVES TRISTRAM, "WE ARE TO BE BLAMED FOR THE MURDER OF VALENTINIAN, FOR HERE COME THE SOLDIERS IN HOT PURSUIT."

"LET'S MEET THEM HERE AND SEND THEIR EARS BACK TO ROME WITH OUR COMPLIMENTS." "NO," SAYS VAL, "NOT WITHIN SIGHT OF THE CITY, ENDLESS RE-ENFORCEMENTS WOULD BE SENT OUT."

"THIS IS THE FIRST TIME MY STEED HAS EVER HEARD THE ENEMY BEHIND HIM," GRUMBLES TRISTRAM, "I CAN JUST FEEL HIS CONTEMPT FOR ME."

A STONE BRIDGE MAKES AN IDEAL SPOT ON WHICH TO HANDLE SUPERIOR NUMBERS AND HERE THEY WAIT FOR THEIR OVER-CONFIDENT PURSUERS.

NEXT WEEK—
Friends Part

194 10-27-40

Prince Valiant

IN THE DAYS OF KING ARTHUR
BY HAROLD R FOSTER

Synopsis: WHEN THE THREE KNIGHTS OF THE ROUND TABLE SAW THE EMPEROR FALL THEY LEFT ROME IMMEDIATELY, FOR THEY KNEW THEY WOULD BE BLAMED FOR THE MURDER. PURSUIT CAME SWIFTLY AND FOR THE FIRST TIME WE SEE KING ARTHUR'S KNIGHTS FLEEING FROM A FOE.

BUT WHEN THEY HAVE LED THEIR PURSUERS OUT OF SIGHT OF THE CITY THEY TURN AND WAIT, RESTING.

THE ROMAN GUARDSMEN EXPECTED TO EASILY OVERCOME THREE FRIGHTENED FOREIGNERS. INSTEAD THEY CRASH INTO IRON LANCE-POINTS, IRON SHIELDS AND IRON MEN!

TRISTRAM GOES INTO THE FRAY SHOUTING, AND HIS WAR-CRY RINGS LIKE A BELL ABOVE THE CLANG OF BATTLE. BRONZE AND IRON; CHAIN AND LEATHER SHEAR OFF LIKE TREE-BARK UNDER THE STROKE OF HIS MIGHTY SWORD.

SIR GAWAIN INFURIATES HIS FOES TO CARELESSNESS BY TAUNTS AND HIGHLY PERSONAL CRITICISM, WHILE HIS TRUSTY SWORD FALLS AMONG THEM LIKE BITTER HAIL.

BUT PRINCE VALIANT LAUGHS GRIMLY THROUGH CLENCHED TEETH; PARRYING WITH SWORD AND SHIELD, STRIKING SELDOM, BUT AT EACH SHREWD, LIGHTNING STROKE ONE LESS ENEMY CONFRONTS THEM.

THE PAMPERED DANDIES OF THE PALACE GUARD STAGGER BACK; THEY ARE NO MATCH FOR THESE TURBULENT SONS OF STORM AND HARDSHIP.

"WITH THIS VICTORY ALL ROME BECOMES OUR ENEMY. WE MUST TURN HOMEWARD WITH ALL SPEED.... AND WE MUST SEPARATE, EACH TO CHOOSE A DIFFERENT DIRECTION; ROME IS TO THE WEST......"
"I CHOOSE EAST, TOWARD THE SEA," SAYS GAWAIN.
"A SEA VOYAGE WILL DO ME GOOD."
"STRAIGHT NORTH AS THE CROW FLIES IS MY CHOICE," SMILES DARK TRISTRAM.
"THEN I GO SOUTH FOR MY HEALTH."

195 11-3-40

THE THREE FRIENDS EMBRACE — PERHAPS FOR THE LAST TIME AND THE TEARS RUN FREELY DOWN THEIR BRONZED CHEEKS...(FOR IN THOSE DAYS BRAVE MEN HAD NOT LEARNED TO BE ASHAMED OF THEIR EMOTIONS.)
NEXT WEEK— **Tristram's Bold Ride.**

Synopsis: NOW HAS COME THE HOUR OF PARTING, FOR THE THREE KNIGHTS OF THE ROUND TABLE HAVE BEEN ACCUSED OF MURDERING THE ROMAN EMPEROR, AND THE PAMPERED DANDIES OF THE PALACE GUARD WHO SOUGHT TO ARREST THEM HAVE BEEN ROUGHLY HANDLED. THEIR ONLY CHANCE NOW IS TO SEPARATE AND TRY TO ESCAPE SINGLY.

TRISTRAM CHOOSES TO RIDE STRAIGHT NORTH, GAWAIN WESTWARD TOWARD THE SEA AND PRINCE VALIANT TO THE SOUTH. "MAY GOOD FORTUNE BRING US ALL TOGETHER AGAIN IN KING ARTHUR'S COURT!"

AND NOW THE TALE TELLS OF TRISTRAM'S BOLD RIDE. THE RIVER TIBER LIES TO THE NORTH AND THE ONLY BRIDGE IS AT ROME,.... SO BACK TO ROME RIDES TRISTRAM!

THE RETREATING SURVIVORS OF THE PALACE GUARD HEAR HIM COMING AND STAND ASIDE.....THEY HAVE HAD QUITE ENOUGH OF THESE TURBULENT NORTHERN KNIGHTS!

AND BOLD TRISTRAM LAUGHS AT THE DANGERS THAT LIE AHEAD; FOR ONCE, BECAUSE OF A DARE, HE HAD ENTERED A WALLED CITY BY NIGHT AND, SINGLE-HANDED, BROUGHT BACK THAT CITY'S KING.

SCARCE AN HOUR SINCE HE LEFT, TRISTRAM RIDES CALMLY BACK. WITHIN THE CITY THERE IS NO EXCITEMENT, SO THE NEWS OF THE EMPEROR'S DEATH HAS NOT YET SPREAD.

BY BACK STREETS AND ALLEYS TRISTRAM SWIFTLY THREADS HIS WAY THROUGH THE GREAT TOWN.

HE FINDS THE BRIDGE, AND NOT A MOMENT TOO SOON, FOR BEHIND HIM ALL THE BELLS ARE TOLLING, ANGRY CRIES RING OUT AND THE SOUND OF MARCHING FEET IS DRAWING CLOSER!

TRISTRAM PLANNED TO HIDE BY DAY AND RIDE SECRETLY BY NIGHT, BUT FINDS TO HIS SURPRISE, THAT ANYONE ACCUSED OF MURDERING THE EMPEROR VALENTINIAN HAS MANY FRIENDS AND HE IS SOON OUT OF DANGER.

SO AT LAST GALLANT TRISTRAM RIDES SAFELY OUT OF OUR STORY AND FOLLOWS HIS HEART BACK TO FAIR ISOLDE IN ENGLAND

NEXT WEEK— *Sir Gawain's Voyage.*

196 11-10-40

Prince Valiant

Synopsis: AS THE WRECKAGE OF WHAT WAS ONCE THE PROUD PALACE GUARD GOES LIMPING BACK TOWARD ROME, TRISTRAM, PRINCE VALIANT AND SIR GAWAIN CAREFULLY WIPE THEIR SWORDS AND PUT THEM AWAY. THEN THEY SAY A QUICK FAREWELL AND GALLOP AWAY, EACH IN A DIFFERENT DIRECTION. FOR THEY ARE AT ODDS WITH THE WHOLE ROMAN EMPIRE AND ONLY BY STEALTH CAN THEY HOPE TO ESCAPE.

AND WESTWARD TOWARD THE SEA GOES GAWAIN, SINGING. FOR THERE IS MORE THAN A HINT OF DANGER IN THE AIR AND DANGER IS AS WINE TO HIS MERRY HEART.

INTO THE SEAPORT TOWN OF OSTIA HE COMES, RIDING HARD, FOR ALREADY THE SIGNAL TOWERS ALONG THE OSTIAN WAY ARE FLASHING A MESSAGE THAT MEANS DEATH TO HIM SHOULD HE TARRY.

RECKLESSLY HE CANTERS ALONG THE CROWDED QUAY, HIS QUICK EYE SEARCHING FOR A DEPARTING SHIP.

HE FINDS ONE ALREADY HEADING FOR THE OPEN SEA AND COMES ABOARD AS ONLY SIR GAWAIN WOULD!

A FAIR PRICE IS OFFERED FOR PASSAGE TO MASSILIA (MARSEILLES), BUT THE CAPTAIN SCENTS A CHANCE FOR EXTORTION AND SAYS— *"NO, WE SAIL FOR CORSE (CORSICA)."* SIR GAWAIN SMILES AND SAYS, *"MASSILIA."*

THE CAPTAIN ASKS TRIPLE THE FARE, HE HINTS AT TURNING BACK, HE THREATENS TO TURN HIM OVER TO THE ROMAN GOVERNOR AT CORSE....BUT SIR GAWAIN-THE-COURTE-OUS ONLY SMILES AND SAYS— *"MASSILIA."*

CAREFULLY GAWAIN PUTS AN EDGE ON HIS GLEAMING SWORD....... *"MASSILIA,"* HE SAYS, STILL SMILING. THE CAPTAIN LOOKS AT THE BRIGHT SMILING EYES, THE GLEAMING WHITE TEETH AND SUDDENLY RE-MEMBERS A PURRING TIGER HE ONCE SAW. THEY SAIL FOR MASSILIA.

THE HOOFBEATS DWINDLE AWAY INTO THE DISTANCE, AS HIS TWO COM-PANIONS RIDE AWAY AND WITH THEM, IT SEEMS, GOES ALL THAT IS BRAVE AND GAY, LEAVING ONLY A LONELY BOY WITH A LUMP IN HIS THROAT. BUT HE SWALLOWS HARD, HIS CHIN COMES UP AND ONCE AGAIN HE IS PRINCE VALIANT, KNIGHT OF THE ROUND TABLE, SPURRING SWIFTLY SOUTHWARD.

NEXT WEEK **Down the Appian Way.**

197 11-17-40

Prince Valiant

IN THE DAYS OF KING ARTHUR
BY
HAROLD R FOSTER

Synopsis: WHEN TRISTRAM, PRINCE VALIANT AND SIR GAWAIN FIND THEY ARE TO BE BLAMED FOR THE MURDER OF THE EMPEROR THEY NOT ONLY LEAVE ROME, BUT GIVE AN ARTISTIC BEATING TO THE GUARDS THAT COME FORTH TO ARREST THEM. THEN THEY SEPARATE, THE BETTER TO ESCAPE THE DETERMINED PURSUIT THEY KNOW WILL FOLLOW.

AS VAL LEAVES THE ROAD AND TURNS SOUTHWARD HE HEARS A CRY BEHIND HIM. *"IT IS I, BOLDORO, YOUR SQUIRE,"* AND THE BLACK-BEARDED ROGUE HE HAD HIRED AS A SERVANT JOINS HIM.

ALL THE OTHER SERVANTS HAD VANISHED DURING THE FIGHT, TAKING THE BAGGAGE WITH THEM, BUT BOLDORO STAYED TO SEE THE FIGHT, PLUNDER THE SLAIN AND THEN JOINS PRINCE VALIANT IN THE HOPE OF MORE LOOT. HE IS A BOLD RASCAL

FOLLOWING THE BANKS OF A SMALL STREAM FLOWING DOWN FROM THE HILLS, THEY FINALLY COME TO THE APPIAN WAY AND TURN TOWARD NAPLES.

FOR TWO DAYS THEY TRAVEL SOUTHWARD UNHINDERED, BUT ON THE THIRD DAY BOLDORO CALLS ATTENTION TO SIGNALS BEING FLASHED FROM TOWER TO TOWER.

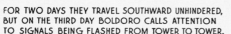

SURE ENOUGH.... AT THE NEXT TOWER SOLDIERS ARE WAITING TO INTERCEPT THEM. THEY TURN OFF THE ROAD AND LOSE THEMSELVES AMONG THE HILLS, TRAVELING ONLY AT NIGHT.

BUT THE HUNT IS ON AND ONCE OR TWICE THEY HEAR ARMED HORSEMEN PASSING IN THE DARKNESS. THE GLOW FROM MT. VESUVIUS GUIDES THEM TOWARD NAPLES.

ONE MORNING THE DAWN COMES QUICKLY AND FINDS THEM FAR FROM ANY HIDING-PLACE. BELOW THEM NAPLES NESTLES AT THE FOOT OF THE SLEEPING VOLCANO. THEN A BUGLE SOUNDS AND A SHOUT GOES UP; THEY HAVE BEEN DISCOVERED!

THEY HAVE TO RUN FOR IT.....AND ROMAN CAVALRY IS SWIFT!

NEXT WEEK - **Into the Volcano.**

198 11-24-40

Prince Valiant

BOLDORO

Registered U.S. Patent Office

Synopsis: THE POLITICIANS OF ROME ARE VERY ANXIOUS TO EXECUTE PRINCE VALIANT FOR THE MURDER OF EMPEROR VALENTINIAN. THE PEOPLE OF ROME ARE ASKING TOO MANY QUESTIONS REGARDING THAT DEED AND A PUBLIC EXECUTION MIGHT SATISFY THEM. BUT VAL IS HARD TO CATCH.

VAL AND BOLDORO MIGHT HAVE EVADED THEIR TIRED PURSUERS AMID THE BROKEN GROUND AT THE FOOT OF MT. VESUVIUS, BUT A FRESH TROOP OF HORSEMEN JOIN THE CHASE AND THEIR CASE BECOMES HOPELESS.

"RIDE ON, BOLDORO, CHANGE OVER OFTEN TO REST THE HORSES.....THEY WILL NOT CHASE YOU AFTER THEY DISCOVER I AM NOT WITH YOU."

HIDDEN AMONG THE ROCKS VAL WATCHES THE ROMAN CAVALRY FLASH BY.

ON A FAR HILLTOP HE SEES THE CAVALRY STOP, TURN AND GALLOP BACK, BUT HE IS FAR UP THE VOLCANO'S SIDE WHERE HORSEMEN CANNOT RIDE.

AND BOLDORO? HE LAUGHED MERRILY! HE NOW HAD JUST THE RIGHT AMOUNT OF EQUIPMENT TO SET HIMSELF UP IN BUSINESS.....HE BECAME A BRIGAND AND, THEY SAY, PROSPERED AMAZINGLY.

BUT VAL'S STRATEGY DOES NOT WORK; THE CAVALRY LEAVE THEIR HORSES AND FOLLOW AFOOT, SPREADING OUT LIKE A NET AND FORCING HIM EVER UPWARD.

BY NIGHTFALL VAL HAS REACHED THE CRATER'S RIM AND PEERS INTO ITS GLOWING HEART. HE HEARS THE SHOUTS OF THE SOLDIERS, AS THEY TOIL SLOWLY UPWARD IN THE DARK AND KNOWS HE MUST GO FORWARD.

HAL FOSTER

DAYLIGHT, AND THE THIRSTY FUGITIVE SEES THE CRATER'S RIM RINGED ABOUT WITH SILENT WATCHERS. SLOWLY THEY DESCEND, HEMMING HIM IN.

NEXT WEEK — **Amid the Smoke.**

199 12-1-40

Prince Valiant

Synopsis: ALL DAY LONG HIS ENEMIES HAVE DRIVEN PRINCE VALIANT HIGHER AND HIGHER UP THE SLOPES OF MT. VESUVIUS. AT NIGHT HE TAKES REFUGE WITHIN THE CRATER, ITSELF   CAPTURE MEANS DEATH AT THE STAKE FOR A CRIME HE NEVER COMMITTED. FURTHER RETREAT OFFERS THE SAME HOT FATE

THE LIGHT OF MORNING REVEALS A RING OF SOLDIERS AROUND THE CRATER'S EDGE.

AS SOON AS IT IS LIGHT ENOUGH A TRUMPET SOUNDS AND THE LEGIONARIES DESCEND IN AN EVER-NARROWING CIRCLE.

SMOKE AND FUMES OBSCURE ONE SECTION OF THE CRATER AND INTO THIS NIGHTMARE WORLD VAL IS FORCED BY THE APPROACHING SOLDIERS.

STILL THEY COME ON, CHOKING, GASPING, AND WITH STREAMING EYES AS THE SULPHUROUS MIST ENVELOPES THEM.

A LOUD METALLIC "CLANK" RINGS OUT, BUT THE SOUND IS DROWNED IN THE RUMBLE AND HISS OF THE VOLCANO.

DISGUISED IN A SOLDIER'S CLOAK AND DENTED HELMET, VAL JOINS THE HUNT, BUT MANAGES TO HANG BACK UNTIL LOST IN THE SWIRLING MIST.   THE LONG CLIMB UP THE CRUMBLING SLOPE, THE STRANGLING FUMES AND BURNING THIRST ARE A TERRIBLE ORDEAL.....BUT LIFE DEPENDS ON IT AND HE WINS THROUGH.

NEXT WEEK—
Out to Sea.

200 12-8-40

HAL FOSTER

Prince Valiant

THE CAPTAIN

Synopsis: FOR THE THIRD TIME PRINCE VALIANT, HAS ESCAPED FROM PURSUING ENEMIES DISGUISED IN THE UNIFORM OF ONE OF THE MORE UNFORTUNATE OF HIS PURSUERS,

BEHIND HIM, ON THE HOT FLOOR OF THE CRATER, THE SOLDIERS ARE STILL SEARCHING, AS VAL GAINS THE RIM.

FAR BELOW, THE BAY OF NAPLES GLITTERS IN THE SUNLIGHT AND STATELY SHIPS GO TO AND FRO..... AND ONE OF THOSE SHIPS MUST CARRY HIM AWAY FROM THESE DANGEROUS SHORES.

VAL MAKES HIS WAY DOWN THE SLOPE AND HIDES AMONG THE VINEYARDS. AT DUSK HE WATCHES THE WEARY SOLDIERS RETURNING FROM THEIR FRUITLESS SEARCH.

WHEN NIGHT FALLS VAL STEALS INTO A FARMYARD AND DRINKS GREEDILY FROM THE WELL, THE FIRST DRINK IN TWO STRENUOUS DAYS.

IN THE DARKNESS HE MAKES HIS WAY TO THE SEA SOME DISTANCE FROM THE WELL-GUARDED WALLS OF NAPLES.

SOME FISHERMEN AGREE TO TAKE HIM OUT WHERE SHIPS PASS. THEY AGREE, BECAUSE IN THESE DAYS IT IS CONSIDERED UNLUCKY TO REFUSE THE REQUEST OF A MAILED AND ARMED WARRIOR.

THROUGH THE MISTS OF MORNING A GRACEFUL SHIP GOES GLIDING BY.

THE SHIP IS BOUND FOR SYRACUSE IN SICILY AND AFTER MUCH HAGGLING, A FARE IS AGREED UPON AND VAL CLIMBS ABOARD.

THERE IS A CRAFTY GLEAM IN THE CAPTAIN'S BEADY EYES...... HIS PASSENGER CAME ABOARD BY STEALTH, HENCE NO ONE KNOWS HE IS ON BOARD, HE WON'T BE MISSED AND THAT PURSE IS HEAVY WITH GOLD AND GEMS.

NEXT WEEK— **The Double-Cross.**

HAL FOSTER

201 12-15-40

Prince Valiant

IN THE DAYS OF
KING ARTHUR
BY
HAROLD R FOSTER

THE CAPTAIN

Synopsis: ON A SHIP BOUND FOR SICILY PRINCE VALIANT ESCAPES FROM HIS ENEMIES IN ROME. MANY NORTHMEN HAVE SETTLED ALONG THE SHORES OF SICILY AND VAL HOPES TO RETURN TO THE NORTH IN ONE OF THEIR VESSELS.

WHILE DREAMING OF HIS DISTANT HOMELAND, VAL IS STARTLED TO HEAR THE CAPTAIN ADDRESSING TWO OF HIS CREW IN THE FAMILIAR TONGUE.

NOT KNOWING THAT THEIR PASSENGER CAN UNDERSTAND EVERY WORD, THEY ARE PLANNING TO GET POSSESSION OF HIS WELL-FILLED PURSE.

"THE NIGHT GROWS CHILLY, WILL YOU JOIN ME IN A WARMING CUP OF WINE?"

"CERTAINLY," AGREES VAL, KNOWING FULL WELL JUST WHY THE CAPTAIN IS SO FRIENDLY.

THE GOBLETS ARE SWITCHED WITH THE GREATEST OF EASE.

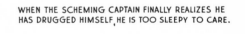

WHEN THE SCHEMING CAPTAIN FINALLY REALIZES HE HAS DRUGGED HIMSELF HE IS TOO SLEEPY TO CARE.

VAL CHANGES CLOAKS AND GOES UP ON DECK.

MISTAKING HIM FOR THE CAPTAIN IN THE DARKNESS, THE TWO ACCOMPLICES WHISPER, *"IS HE ASLEEP?"* FOR ANSWER VAL JINGLES HIS PURSE.

202 12-22-40.

AND SO IT IS THE CAPTAIN WHO, ACCORDING TO HIS OWN PLAN, IS BORNE TOWARD THE RAIL.

NEXT WEEK **The Approaching Storm.**

HAL FOSTER

Synopsis: IF PRINCE VALIANT EXPECTED A RESTFUL VOYAGE TO SICILY, HE WAS VERY MUCH MISTAKEN, FOR NO SOONER HAD THE RASCALLY CAPTAIN SEEN THE WEIGHT OF VAL'S PURSE THAN HE TRIED TO DRUG HIS WINE. VAL SWITCHES THEIR GOBLETS, AND LATER, THEIR CLOAKS.

THE TWO SAILORS CARRY OUT THE CAPTAIN'S ORDERS........ AND THE CAPTAIN!

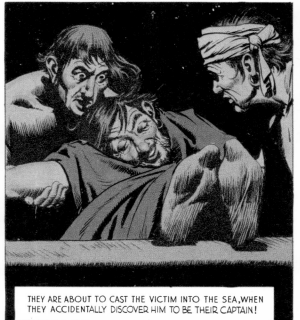

THEY ARE ABOUT TO CAST THE VICTIM INTO THE SEA, WHEN THEY ACCIDENTALLY DISCOVER HIM TO BE THEIR CAPTAIN!

THAT HARD SMILE AND THAT ALL-TOO-BRIGHT SWORD ARE NOT VERY RE-ASSURING TO A GUILTY CONSCIENCE.

VAL MAKES THEM RETURN THE CAPTAIN TO THE CABIN, BUT ALL EFFORTS TO REVIVE HIM FAIL .... HIS OWN DRUG IS VERY EFFECTIVE.

VAL CAREFULLY PUTS ASIDE HIS SWORD......THEN, BREAKING THE LEG FROM A STOOL, POINTS OUT HOW WRONG IT IS TO TRIFLE WITH A WARRIOR.

COMING UP ON DECK, VAL FINDS THE SHIP PITCHING UNEASILY BEFORE A GATHERING STORM.

WITH THE CAPTAIN AND HIS TWO OFFICERS UNFIT FOR SERVICE, A STORM APPROACHING AND PANIC SPREADING AMONG THE CREW, VAL TAKES CHARGE....HE IS OBEYED, FOR HE POINTS OUT HIS ORDERS WITH A SWORD!

WITH SHORTENED SAIL THEY GO SCUDDING BEFORE THE SCREAMING WIND, NOT KNOWING WHAT MAY LIE AHEAD IN THE DARKNESS.

NEXT WEEK— **Past Scylla and Charybdis.**

203 12-29-40

IN OUR NEXT VOLUME:

PRINCE VALIANT

VOL. 3: 1941-1942

This volume leads off with the epic ten-month saga of Val's globe-trotting search for Aleta through Northern Africa, with stops in Jerusalem, the Arabic deserts (including an eye-popping visit to a harem), and ultimately the "Misty Isles." But their romance is not destined to be (at least not yet) and so a disappointed, even embittered Val wends his eventful way back to Camelot — encountering en route a man destined to become a lifelong friend, the boisterous Viking Boltar. Then an alliance of Vikings and Picts threatens Britain's security and it's off on another journey…

Available at all good bookstores Christmas 2010!